With love & bliss,

Love,
Mommy

Love, Mommy

WRITING LOVE LETTERS TO YOUR BABY

JUDY SIBLIN-LIBRACH

ECW Press

Published by ECW PRESS 2120 Queen Street East, Suite 200, Toronto,
Ontario, Canada M4E 1E2

LIBRARY AND ARCHIVES CANADA CATALOGUING IN PUBLICATION

Siblin-Librach, Judy
Love, Mommy : writing love letters to your baby / Judy
Siblin-Librach.
ISBN 978-1-55022-758-1
1. Mother and child. 2. Letter writing. 3. Parenting. I. Title.
HQ779.S52 2007   305.232   C2006-906796-1

Editor: Jennifer Hale
Cover and text design: Tania Craan
Production: Mary Bowness
Front cover photo: Tracy Kahn/Corbis
Author photo: J. Michael La Fond, www.lafondphoto.com
Printing: Transcontinental

This book is set in Sabon

With the publication of *Love, Mommy* ECW PRESS acknowledges the
generous financial support of the Government of Canada through the
Book Publishing Industry Development Program (BPIDP) for our
publishing activities. Canadä

DISTRIBUTION

CANADA: Jaguar Book Group, 100 Armstrong Ave.,
Georgetown, ON L7G 5S4
UNITED STATES: Independent Publishers Group,
814 North Franklin St., Chicago, IL 60610

Printed and bound in Canada

ECW PRESS
ecwpress.com

To Max and Lily — the loves of my life

and

to Cliff, for making all of my dreams come true.

table of contents

How It All Began

AS I WRITE THIS, I HAVE JUST put my daughter Lily to bed. I look at her lying there with her golden curls tousled all over her pillow and I can't believe she's five-and-a-half years old. Yesterday, I watched my son Max at his eighth birthday party, playing hockey in the rain. He was surrounded by all of his friends and he looked so happy. And so tall. Now it's school and programs and never-ending playdates. I remember when it was just us together. What happened? And so while I'm happy, I also feel sad, because it's happening far too quickly. It just confirms for me that I'm doing the right thing in writing this book.

I know I'm not the first mother and I'm sure I won't be the last to have been swept right off my feet by the sheer joy and passion of motherhood. Even though I asked mothers, friends, and relatives about what it would really be like, no amount of description, however evocative, could prepare me for the magic and majesty of it all. I just know that very early on when my first child Max was born, and later my daughter Lily, I felt overwhelmed with love, and it felt like it was all spilling over.

If I were a painter I would have splashed paint all over a canvas to describe the kaleidoscope of emotions I was feeling. If I were a dancer, I would have created some choreography and leapt my way into understanding. But I am a writer, and so writing it down seemed to be the most natural thing to do.

At first, it had no form. It was just a ball of emotions and perceptions, thoughts and feelings, like the dough we start with when we're baking bread. And while I struggled intensely with putting all of these wonderful feelings into words, one thing became clear: I wanted my son and later my daughter to know in no uncertain terms how I felt about them, and this was a way to begin expressing that love.

So I took that clump of dough and as I shaped it, kneaded it, braided it, and looked at it with fresh eyes, I realized that what I really was doing was writing a love letter to my children.

Why a love letter, you may be wondering. Isn't that something we write when we're "in love," in a romantic relationship as it were? All I can tell you is that so many mothers I've talked to have described this as a love unlike any other. It is an unconditional love, a holy love — whatever it is, once it grips you and gets hold of your heart, your life is transformed forever. Why *not* write about that?

Chronicling the precious memories of your children is priceless, because you are giving them back a piece of their memory that they otherwise wouldn't have access to. Kids are forever asking, "What was I like when I came home from the hospital? What was I like when I was little?" Children love to hear these stories, and they crave information about what happened when they were small and they can't remember without your help. So many mothers have said to me, "I could kick myself for not writing these stories down." But inevitably we don't. We're too busy, we're tired, we're multi-tasking and writing letters to our children might seem daunting. But it isn't. It's actually lots of fun, instantly gratifying, a feeling-good lift for you and your child and something you'll never regret.

And it's never too late.

The good news is, whether you're a new parent, a mother- or father-to-be, or a parent looking back, or even a grandparent, you can make those moments come alive again by capturing them with words.

So "let me be your memory" became an exciting possibility. I wanted to be Max and Lily's memory, so that if they were ever lost along the way, these letters, these little glimpses into their early personalities, might be the lamp they would need to light their way back home.

These letters can be *your* lamp as well. They are not only the most precious gift you can give to your children, they're also a gift to yourself. Because one day when they go off to college or get married, rereading these letters will help you relive some of the happiest times of your life. They can become your solace and comfort as your children go off to spread their wings and become independent.

Maybe I'm writing this because like you, I love these children so much that I want them to know how magnificent they are and that there's someone in this world who loves them just because, and they don't have to do anything but just be, and they're perfect just the way they are.

I want to tell them about all of the other people in their lives who were so important to them, and always will be, and I've encouraged other family members to put down their memories of Max and Lily to add to my letters. I am so blessed to have married Cliff, a fertility specialist who has helped create hundreds and hundreds of babies, but when our Max and Lily were born, the world stopped for him, too, and he finally got to experience the same joy and the same miracle that he has been able to bring to others. Because of the demands of his job, he doesn't get the pleasure of spending as much time with Max and Lily as I can. But he, too, is writing letters to them, and while they know how much he adores them, these letters will always remind them of his immense love for them.

So I have memories — there's Max getting on the yellow school bus. Oh, wait a minute, there's Lily going off to camp for the first time with her lunch box in her little hands, wearing a pink hat that's so big it covers her entire face. And oh, oh, yes, just a minute, there's a glimpse of Max standing alone in the schoolyard — will a friend come over to play with him? And there's Lily, walking shyly into her ballet class for the first time.

And we want to protect them and make it all right and make their lives as perfect as they've made ours.

But we can't. We can only love them and guide them and give them everything they might need on this journey they're on from the moment we meet them for the very first time.

So maybe I'm writing this so I can have that little bit of security to hold on to the details and the nuances of the happiest moments of my life.

And so I wait until the bus pulls away, my face aching from the smile I put on so they'll be happy as they're driving off, and when I can't see the bus any longer, that's when I cry. Because I'm weeping for what was and will never be quite the same again. But by writing it down, we can at least have a sweet and delicious reminder that this beautiful time really did happen.

Gestation

How You Can Do It, Too

SO HOW CAN YOU DO IT? I'll never forget when I was giving a workshop on my book, and a simple story like the first time I gave my son a bath opened the floodgates of memory in the participants. I followed the reading with the question, "What was the moment when you knew you had become a mother for sure and there was no going back?" Boxes of Kleenex, lots of laughs and hours later, everyone emerged from the workshop cleansed, uplifted, and reminded of the best part of their lives.

And so, there it was! The final piece fell into place. Getting *you* to write letters to your babies is what I most want to accomplish with this labor of love. Ideally, you will write your letters to your babies when they are babies. That's how you're most likely to capture all the details. But don't worry if your kids are a little older, you can still reach back into your memory and capture on paper what it was like when they were in your minute-by-minute care. It's never too late.

Now the first thing most people think when asked

to write something is, "But I can't write. I'm not a writer." But there is only one person your children want to hear from: *you*, their mommy, or daddy, not some Shakespearian genius or acclaimed *New York Times* best-selling author. Your children want to hear your voice, your tone, and your words, and that way they can have you close to them forever.

Before each one of my letters, which I use as examples for you, there will be a note to moms and dads about how you can write the letter, along with some writing tips and suggestions to get you motivated and inspired. These notes will act as a prompt to stimulate your memory and imagination as you recall similar events with your children and begin to write them down. I will then include an example of a letter I wrote to one of my children.

Following each letter is a short statement called "The Magic Key," a nugget extracted from the letter that captures something particular about the child or the incident being described. They are often one or more of the following:

- ♥ An *insight* into a central characteristic or personality trait revealed by the baby during those precious early years.
- ♥ A *compliment* that goes right to the being of the child.
- ♥ A *reminder* of who they really are.
- ♥ A word of *inspiration* to help them carry on in spite of life's trials.
- ♥ A word of *motherly or fatherly wisdom or advice* that will open up rich possibilities in their lives as they grow.

What all the Magic Keys have in common is that they are a lovely way of noticing and acknowledging something treasured about the children that makes them so special, both in their very being and in your relationship to them. In fact, if you were to list all these keys on a page, you would have a summary of the nature of your child that says: together, these keys unlock your very essence and this is why I love you so much — as if I needed any reason at all.

This may be the central point of this book. As a mom I've had the pleasure of having lots of kids in our home since my children were babies. We've had a school in our house, lots of music groups, playdates, parties, and sleepovers, and everyone calls our house "playgroup central." What I have seen both with my children and all of their friends is that kids really thrive and blossom when they're noticed. Children have a wish to be seen and heard and acknowledged and by writing these letters and especially the Magic Keys, we are realizing that wish and elevating their spirit. We are consciously acknowledging what we cherish about their unique qualities, characteristics, and special gifts. They love this and they flourish when we shine this light on them.

I am a child of divorce. From the tender age of three I was involved in shuttle diplomacy between my father's and mother's houses. I suppose psychologists might call it overcompensation on my part, but maybe this is why I have been so motivated to give my children the warm, close, happy, and deeply safe and loving family I never had. Every time I notice them by giving them love and attention, opportunity, affirmation, and belief in themselves, I feel such profound joy. Just seeing the happiness on their faces and knowing that they feel so loved, safe, and secure has definitely healed many of the hurts and taken a lot of the pain away.

After some of the Magic Keys, I will include an example or two of another parent writing about his or her child, to show how different one story can be to two different people. You can do the same thing with your letters: ask your partner, a grandparent, or a caregiver to include their version of the same story, to give your child more than one perspective.

You may not use all these devices in your letters, but no matter how you construct them, there's one key thing to remember: you are writing *love letters* to your babies.

Love letters are always cherished. Who doesn't love waiting for a love letter, the anticipation of reading it and then the joy of knowing that they are adored and that someone took the time to write to them. Love letters are often saved in special places, like in a keepsake chest, jewelry box, or even in a heart-shaped chocolate box or old shoebox, tucked away in a dresser drawer, or in an old-fashioned trunk up in an attic. They are often tied with pretty ribbon and then placed in a hope chest and are lovingly revisited for years to come. Over time, the letters may become worn and faded, but the words remain as true as the day they were written.

So I hope you will enjoy the love letters I have written to my babies, Max and Lily. I *know* you will enjoy writing love letters to yours.

Pregnancy

When You Were in My Tummy

WHAT CAN YOU TELL YOUR CHILD about what it was like for you when they were in your tummy? Was there one characteristic that your child revealed to you even before they were born? How did your partner react during the pregnancy? Did he touch your tummy? Did he play music? Did you look at early ultrasounds? How did you find out you were pregnant? Were you trying for a long time? Involve your partner in this one and get them to write a letter of what it was like when their child was in Mommy's tummy and their recollections of getting pickles and ice cream, or massaging Mommy's tummy, talking to the baby, and just watching this miracle happen.

Did you want to know the sex of your children before they were born? If so, what do remember about that discovery? And if you didn't find out before, what was it like when the doctor or midwife announced the sex of your baby?

Dear Lily,

Before I even knew I was pregnant with you, Lily, I had a really incredible experience where I was driving along a side street and all of a sudden I stopped. I remember having this moment where I put my hand over my mouth and I suddenly knew that I was pregnant and I was having a girl. Sure enough, when we did the pregnancy test that evening, I was indeed pregnant, but the rest was still a mystery.

When I was pregnant the first time, I really didn't want to know the sex of my baby, because I wanted the surprise. But this time was different. I really wanted to know and I really wanted a girl.

About three months later, I had my amnio. The next three weeks of waiting for the results seemed interminable. Finally, one Monday morning on my way to buy sixteen chocolate cupcakes for Max and his classmates for his second-year class birthday party at his nursery school, I called my answering machine and heard this message from my obstetrician, Dr. Cohen. I heard his familiar voice saying, "I have the results to your amnio. Please call me back."

What to do? It was already 9:15 and Max's party was starting in fifteen minutes. I had already waited for three weeks, what were two more hours? And, I knew that if I called the doctor back right away, I would miss the whole birthday party. So I dredged up every ounce of willpower I could muster and took Max to his class party. Max was not into the Barney party at all that day and being very shy, he didn't like all of that attention on him and he really wanted out of there. I didn't want to hurt the teacher's feelings, so I just waited it out and the minute it was over, we bolted out of there and went back to the parking lot. I put Max in his car seat and debated about what I should do. Should I call now or wait until I got home? A brother for Max would be a good thing, I told myself. But I wanted a girl so badly, I can't begin to tell you. I wanted a little girl so I could name her after Grandma Siblin, another precious Lily.

I couldn't stand it anymore. I picked up the phone and called Dr. Cohen's office. Only he wasn't there. His nurse said he had left for the day. What? It was impossible. This was total torture. I couldn't even respond. Silence.

I finally mustered, "He's gone for the day?"

"Yes, he is gone for the day," she repeated. "May I have him call you back tomorrow?"

"Oh," I finally answered, "I'm just returning his call."

"Well, that's good," she said. "May I have your name?"

"It's Judy Librach," I answered. "It's regarding the amnio."

"Oh, why didn't you say so? I have those results, would you like them?"

I hesitated. Should I find out now? Should I wait for Cliff? Should I wait and be surprised like I did with Max? No, I had to know, and I had to know right away.

"Yes, I would like the results please," I finally managed.

"Well," she said. "Everything is good and your baby

is healthy. Would you care to know the sex?"

"Yes, I would," I answered, holding my breath and crossing my fingers, my heart beating a mile a minute.

"Well, you're going to have a beautiful baby girl."

"What did you say?" I asked, not trusting my ears.

"You're having a girl," she repeated.

"Are you sure? Absolutely sure?" I said.

Then the tears started. I cried so hard, I couldn't stop. I felt so much relief flooding through me.

Finally the nurse asked, "This is good news, isn't it?"

"Oh, yes, it's great news," I answered. "It's the best news in the world. I'm sorry, I'm just so happy."

Hanging up the phone, I put my head on the steering wheel and wept and wept until finally Max said, "Are you okay, Mommy? Why are you crying? Are you sad?"

"I'm not sad, Max, I'm so happy. Mommy's just crying because she's so happy. You're going to have a little sister."

So, Lily, that's how I found out I was having a girl, and that girl was you. And it was definitely one of the happiest moments of my life.

Love, Mommy

The Magic Key: Lemons and balsamic vinegar really do work if you want to have a girl. But seriously, you were loved and anticipated from the very beginning, more than you'll ever know.

Every parent has the same, but different, experience of pregnancy:

Alison: "The incredible thing that I noticed with Casey is that he would move all the time in my belly. And I just found that interesting that he moved in my sleep, almost like he danced and he moved his arms like he was dancing. He moved his whole body as if he was always dancing and I'd never seen another child do that. He really started dancing at conception, in utero. So I was not surprised that he came out and he still looked like he was dancing. When he was lying in his chair, he always moved like he was dancing. He was always moving when he was sleeping. My other two are very still when they sleep. So when I started him in dance when he was four, I wasn't surprised that he took to it so readily. And he demanded from me that I put him in a real structure and he is now twelve years old and has been been at the National Ballet of Canada since he was six. He was in *La Sylphide* last month and now at Christmastime, this will be his fifth year of dancing in *The Nutcracker.*"

Similar topics:

♥   Having an amniocentesis
♥   Did you want to know the sex of your baby?
♥   Did you keep your early ultrasound photos?
♥   Memories of the baby kicking for the first time
♥   Shopping for maternity clothes

Starting to Write Your Letters — This is a great place to start writing love letters to your children, because we all have a memory of what it was like at the very beginning, when you were first pregnant and carrying your child or watching your spouse or partner carrying your child. So, if you are a new mother or father and are reading this book as you go through the experience, you may want to try keeping a journal or a diary about the new experiences you have every day. In fact, whether you're a new mother, a mother-to-be, a mother or grandmother looking back, this is a perfect place to begin.

You don't have to strive for perfection in the first telling. Just let it out, like a sculptor does when they first craft a piece of art. You can go back after and add the finishing touches and the glazes and paint it and bake it. For now you just want to reiterate the story and try to remember as many details as you can when they're still fresh and new. The rest will all come together. You can contextualize the era as well: What else was going on in the world at the time? What music was popular? What television shows or movies were people watching? What major world events were happening at the time?

The Birth

The Happiest Moment of My Life

WHAT ARE THE MOST POSITIVE and happy things that happened for you in your birth experience? In our culture we often talk abut the negatives or the high dramas of it, instead of the beauty and the joy of it all, and that is what you want to remember fifty years from now. So let that be your starting point.

How would you describe to your child what it was like giving birth to them? What did you love about it? Try this exercise: Pretend that you are writing a paragraph in a book that totally describes your birth experience for someone who is never going to meet you and will only know what it was like for you from that one paragraph. What would that paragraph say? Were you excited? Nervous? Was it what you expected, totally different, or something in between? What were you like during it all? What was most comforting and least comforting? What gave you strength? Did you dance, pray, breathe? Did you do everything you learned in your prenatal class, or did you rely purely on instinct? Did you bring pictures or any items to soothe you or help you through the experience? Did you have pain relief? Go back to the beginning. Were you on time, or past your due date? Did you deliver in hospital or at home? And if in hospital, what do you remember about the ride to the hospital? How did you feel before, during, and after the delivery? How did your partner react? How did family members react? If you had to describe this to your child in twenty-five words or less, what would you write? What are your reflections and favorite moments and memories of the glorious event? What about your partner's recollections?

And you can't talk about the ride *to* the hospital without including the ride home *from* the hospital. In that space of time between exiting the car in labor and then reentering it with a baby, our lives are completely changed. What was it like the day you and your baby came home from the hospital? What was the weather like? Was it morning or afternoon? How did you feel on the ride home? Was it a peaceful ride? How did the world look to you? Who was there to greet you? What did you do first? How did you feel when you walked into the house with your new baby? What are your memories of your baby on their first day at home?

Dear Max,
The big day finally arrived. I was admitted into hospital on October 27, 1997. You were one week overdue. My doctor decided to induce me and bring

darling you into this world.

It was nothing like I expected. I found that giving birth to you was something of a spiritual experience for me, and I think Daddy would agree. It was very beautiful and so much easier than the books or other mothers had described.

Daddy was great, a prince: so kind, so loving and so "there" with me while we waited for your arrival. I've never loved him more in my entire life. During labor we slow-danced to the music that Daddy and I had fallen in love to — Michael Jones's instrumental piano recordings, *Pianoscapes*. The music was passionate, deep and beautiful, just like our experience of each other.

We had a lovely lady with us, Alison, who among other things works as a labor coach. She worked magically with Daddy and me, massaging my back, reminding me to breathe, and helping me to relax. Alison loves what she does so much. She loves babies and pregnant mothers and watching and helping to bring new life into the world. She was cheerful and loving but no-nonsense, and so earnest in her desire to be there with us that she created an environment in that room that made it so special for you, Max, to be born into that room and that energy. She possessed that unique ability to be present when needed, without being obtrusive. So even Daddy, who had been so reluctant to have her in the first place, was so happy that she was part of it all.

At one point I said to Daddy and Alison, "I feel like we are in a symphony together, all of us playing our instruments and bringing them together to make beautiful music." It was really like that, Max. It was a very magical journey bringing you into this world.

Between contractions, we listened to a relaxation tape that I had had for years. I don't know the exact name of it, because the label has been blurred by years of use. But I do remember a very relaxed male voice with a distinct South African accent. He said things like: "Begin by getting relaxed. Get as comfortable as you can. Switch off all the responses all over your body as your muscles begin to ease off further and further. Now take in a deep breath, right in, and already you should be able to feel a calmer sensation developing. More and more. Further and further."

I tried to visualize calm and serene thoughts. And indeed, with the help of the tape, I got into a very relaxed state. Well, not only did I relax, but so did Daddy and the nurses, and even the doctor. He finally said: "Please turn that thing off, Judy, it's making me fall asleep." We all had a good laugh over that one.

About seven hours into my labor, I had an epidural, which gave me a break, and I drifted off while Daddy slept soundly beside me. What I didn't expect was the spiritual component that made the whole thing one of the greatest epiphanies of my life. Even the pain. Everything had a purpose and a meaning. Everything made sense, even the pain. Because I knew that at the end of it all, I'd have the greatest thing on this earth, which of course, was you.

Grandma Barbara arrived towards the end of my labor and she was there while I was pushing. Daddy stood beside me stoically and at one point, Grandma

How to Keep Going — Make a writing date with yourself and keep the appointment. If you had a doctor or a dentist appointment, you probably wouldn't cancel it. So honor the time you put aside to do the writing. Find a space all of your own, even if it's just putting up a screen in your bedroom to create a little writing nook. I remember writing at my desk while Max, at five months old, played happily in a playpen beside me. We would wile away the hours together listening to music, him playing, and me writing beside him. Find the time during the day when you are "at your best" and are the most refreshed, invigorated, and ready to write and then just do it! You won't regret it.

Barbara said, "Why don't you sit down for a while, Cliff?" Daddy smiled politely but answered: "If Judy can do all the work she's doing, I want to show her my support by being at her side."

He didn't budge from his spot for almost three hours. He was resolute, focused, standing at the end of the bed as if he was on the front lines, a captain, head of the troops, and he wasn't going to let me or the country down. When I asked, "Cliff, how am I doing?" he answered, "Honey, you have to ask the doctor. Today, I'm just a husband, and a father."

You were born at 6:59 a.m. on October 28, 1997. But I couldn't hear the doctor tell me whether you were a boy or a girl because Grandma Barbara was crying so loudly. Then I heard someone say you were a boy. Maxwell Jules. That was the name Daddy and I had already picked out for you. I loved you instantly.

That day all of your family from Montreal came to welcome you to the world: Grandpa Siblin, Auntie Jane, and Grandma Jackie. Auntie Jane crawled right into bed with me to share my joy and be close to you. She fell in love with you right away, too, and said that although she couldn't possibly feel exactly as I did, she felt a pretty close second in her love of you, her beloved little nephew. Everyone who came to see you couldn't believe how perfect you were. When Grandpa held you in his arms, he had such a look of tenderness on his face, I wanted to cry. You were so new, and already had so much love.

Max, the day you were born was the happiest day of my life. It all went by so quickly and two days later I couldn't believe that it was time to take you home already. We dressed you up in your blue terrycloth sleeper and your baby blue-and-white fleece jacket, and your tiny navy-blue-and-white car seat. Then we bundled you up in lots of little blankets. Finally we put on your little white mittens and a wee little hat — you looked so cute! Your cousin Zachary used to tease me about how much I bundled you, particularly when I was still doing it nine months later, in July.

We lifted you up and put you carefully inside the backseat of Daddy's car, facing you towards the back. I got into the backseat beside you where I would continue to sit for years to come. And I said to Daddy, "Please drive carefully. He's so fragile. He's like a little egg." Driving home was the most surreal experience of my life.

The streets looked different. The trees looked different, almost as if I'd never seen them before. The whole world looked different and it was because you were here now. Before we were only living a lifestyle, now, we were beginning our lives. We couldn't wait to get you home.

We brought you upstairs to your little yellow-and-white room and changed your diaper and put you in a little bassinet. And I nursed you in your rocking chair while we played what would become your favorite tape for the next three years afterwards. The tape was "The Rockabye Lullabye Collection." And you fell fast asleep. And we were so happy that you were home at last!

Love, Mommy

Here are some of Daddy's memories of your birth:

Dear Max,

I was very impressed with Mommy's bravery and how she went all the way to five centimeters dilated before receiving any pain relief. I recall during the contractions putting our arms around each other tightly and breathing and dancing through the contractions together. And when Mommy was pushing you out, I was amazed at how determined she was even after hours of pushing and how she found the strength to keep going. And when the doctor helped pull you out, I couldn't believe you were actually here. After seeing so many babies born from my patients, I never thought it would seem so special when it was my own child. How wrong I was. I was immediately bonded to you like no other person in the world. And I couldn't stop staring at you and couldn't believe that you came from the two of us.

Love, Daddy

The Magic Key: When I see you and Daddy both being calm and stoic, you are so much alike and I'm in love with you both even more. The key is to take that love and that beautiful energy you possess and light up others. And in doing so, the light will shine right back on you. Always know that you were so wanted and so welcome that you were like royalty arriving at your palace.

If you have more than one child, tell them about the difference between their birth and their sibling's:

Dear Lily,

It was completely different when I gave birth to you. For one, it was a lot shorter; the pushing took only forty-five minutes instead of the three hours it had been with your brother. I just remember everyone laughing so much. I practically delivered you myself, because Dr. Cohen encouraged me to pull you up to me after he delivered your little shoulders. So our eyes locked right away and there was so much love between us. And you nursed right away, too, unlike Max who went right into the baby incubator. He also didn't cry for the first few minutes and you cried right away. Daddy said you wanted Mommy to know that you were okay. I felt such a tug at my heart when I saw you for the first time. It was as if it we'd known each other and this was the beginning of a magical and very close relationship that we would share together for a very long time. I couldn't get over how protective I felt, like I just wanted to hold you close to me and protect you from the world. Forever.

You were named after my late grandma Siblin, who had been the love of my life. I loved you so much already and I didn't even know you yet. I was amazed by the intensity of my feelings for you. A daughter, and that daughter is you. What a dream come true.

Love, Mommy

You can write separate letters to each child, or combine them in one letter to all of them:

Carrie: Mommy has gone through labor three times! First with Reith, then with Hunter, and finally with Keagan. Hunter was the hardest. Weighing in at 9 lb. 8 oz., it was the only time Mommy wished that maybe she took something for the pain. Being able to go through labor without medicated assistance though just makes Mommy appreciate her three boys even more.

Reith, when you were born, you couldn't breathe at first because the umbilical cord had wrapped around your neck twice. The doctor quickly got you free though and disappeared for an hour to get you breathing and make sure you were okay.

Hunter, you had a very quick heartbeat which caused concern. The nurse removed you for three long hours. They asked Mommy to try to get some rest, but Mommy was told you would only be gone for an hour and was becoming desperate to see you when two more hours had gone by. Mommy was very relieved to see you when the nurse finally brought you back to me. You, like Reith, were also fine.

Keagan, Mommy used a midwife this time around and almost waited too long at home while in labor. We made it to the hospital at 10:10 a.m. The other two midwives waited to have her head midwife come and break Mommy's water at 10:30 a.m. and seven minutes later you were born! They made sure to place you on Mommy's chest right after. They even let Mommy cut your umbilical cord! Unless there was a real problem, they weren't going to take you away from Mommy as quickly as your two older brothers had been. It was the best labor and delivery of all three.

Adoption

Babies all arrive into our arms in different ways. So if your child grew in your heart and not in your tummy, there are many wonderful, happy, and exciting stories to tell them about how you met them for the first time. Tell them where they came from, how much you wanted a baby, the happy parts of the adoption process, seeing your baby for the first time, and what it was like bringing him or her home.

Samantha:

Dear David,

You arrived on the scene about a month earlier than you were supposed to. Daddy and I thought we had plenty of time to get ready for your arrival. We had already met your birth families — parents and grandparents on both sides — and had expected to be packed and organized in plenty of time to get there for your birth.

Well, it seems you had other plans.

One afternoon, just over a month before you were supposed to be born, I got a phone call. It was your birth mother's mother. She said, "You'd better get down here as soon as possible, because the baby is going to be born today!"

I was so excited — and so frantic. I phoned Daddy at work. He came home right away. We threw everything into the van and drove for ten hours straight, hoping to get there in time.

We didn't make it. You arrived about five hours before we did. But you know what? It didn't really matter. When we got to the hospital, we knocked on the door of your birth mother's room.

"Come in," she said, in a soft voice.

She was sitting up in bed, holding you. You were all wrapped up, like a little burrito. Daddy and I came close to the bed, and your birth mother slipped you into my arms.

"Here's your baby," she said.

Then she cried, and we cried, because we were all

so happy that you were ours and that we were going to be a family.

Similar topics:

♥ Your baby's nursery
♥ Preparations for the baby's arrival
♥ Your other children's reactions to the new baby
♥ Reactions of first-time grandparents
♥ Flowers, gifts, cards, and e-mails

The Moment I Knew
I Was a Mom

WHAT WAS THE MOMENT WHEN you knew you had become a mother or father and there was no going back? This is one of the questions that always elicits a very emotional and visceral reaction from the moms at the workshops I lead. Answering this question also becomes not only a defining moment for you as a parent, but a defining moment for what your relationship is going to be with this little person.

Every mother has that "moment" when she knows she's become a mother, and everything suddenly becomes real. You know what I'm talking about. Your love for this little being grabs a hold of you, stirring something inside of your heart and taking on a life of its own. In this moment you finally realize you are bonded, connected, joined together for life, and now this little being *is* your life, and you wonder how you ever lived without them. You finally understand what all those people were talking about when they told you that your life would change completely.

Some mothers have said it happens the first time they nurse their baby, or the first time they have to leave their child and the pangs they experience while they're away, even if it's for a short while. Others have said it happens the first time their child is sick and they realize how needed they are. It might be at one of those five-o'clock-in-the-morning feedings, when it's just you and your child and that quiet and peacefulness all around you.

Describe that moment. Where were you, what happened, how did you feel, and what made it so special?

For me, it was when I gave my son, Max, a bath for the very first time.

Dear Max,

It was early evening in November 1997. We were upstairs in our old house, and all was very quiet. Daddy was out delivering a baby. The time had come to do what I had been dreading the most: give you a bath for the first time all by myself.

All of the magic of your newness was everywhere — your sweet smell, your angelic sounds, the warm, cozy aura around you. I had a heightened sense of your presence throughout the house at all times. I felt like all of my senses were acutely alive. That night something that should have been so simple — giving you a bath — had taken on monumental proportions.

How could something as commonplace be so frightening? What if you slipped out of my hands and I dropped you? What if I forgot everything I'd learned in my prenatal class when we bathed the plastic doll in the pretend bathtub with lots of other first-time mothers and fathers watching over their pretend plastic dolls? What if this, what if that? I don't know why I was so afraid. Maybe I didn't trust myself to do something so important. This was, after all, *you* we were talking about, the most important little person in our house.

Until then, Auntie Pearl, had always given you your bath while I watched on the sidelines, marvelling at the ease and effortless grace she used to get you into the football hold and maneuver you in and out of the water. As I ran the water, I couldn't get this image out of my mind: Auntie Pearl draping you over her hip, carrying extra towels, washcloths, receiving blankets, and a shampoo bottle in her free hand. During all of this she still managed to sing songs and look totally relaxed and at ease as if you were just a part of her body. Would I ever feel that comfortable, or be that relaxed about it all?

I also knew that you never liked being bathed in the first place. As loving and wonderful as Auntie Pearl was, every time she gave you a bath, you would cry your heart out. I found it so painful to you hear you cry like that. It made me feel so helpless. So, naturally, I assumed you would cry uncontrollably when I gave you your bath for the first time.

Auntie Pearl was preparing to go home to her family and she put her hands on her hips and said in her loving but no-nonsense way, "Enough is enough. You're on your own." So while I still had her, I followed her around for days and wrote everything down in a note-book. Until recently, the little book was still in your diaper bag — somewhat dog-eared but still a great little guide for anyone in need of a Newborn Baby 101 intro-ductory course.

What was in there? Everything. Every time she bathed or diapered you, I made little notes and com-ments and gave them headings like "How to Change His Diaper" and "How to Give Him a Real Bath" (as opposed to a sponge bath, which was on another page). You get into this mother mode and it doesn't matter if you were running a corporation or saving lives, all of a sudden you don't know anything and you have to learn everything all over again.

So the time had finally come. In we went to the bath-room. I filled your little white plastic bathtub halfway with warm water and tested it countless times. In my head, I rehearsed the order that things should be done in: "Wet washcloth first. Wash face. Drizzle water over hair with washcloth. Squeeze out tiny amount of baby shampoo." Then I braced myself for the rinsing part. I was afraid I would get soap in your eyes or that you would be frightened, or worse still, hurt. So I painstak-ingly squeezed the water out of the washcloth over the back of your head, then slowly over the sides and the front until all the soap was gone. Another milestone.

Hands trembling, but nevertheless feeling encour-aged by our success thus far, I began the most frightening part of the bath. Gently holding the back of your little head with my right hand and supporting the rest of your body with my left hand and my prayers, I lowered you into the tub.

Suddenly I realized something: You weren't crying! You weren't scared! This was the first time you hadn't cried during your bath! Instead, you looked at me so calmly and so sweetly. Your eyes never left me for a moment. I felt like you were helping me, supporting me in a way, and silently trusting me with all of your little heart.

Feeling almost giddy with relief, I began bundling you in your towel, saying silently, "I can do this. I think he likes it, bless his little heart." So I laid the towel on my chest as I'd learned, put the hood over your head, and wrapped you up in a little bundle.

In we went to your nursery and began your after-bath routine. First I sprinkled cornstarch on your tummy and just under your chin for freshness. I applied your diaper-rash cream and then gently massaged your chest and legs with mineral oil. Carefully, I slipped your little arms into your undershirt and finally put on your soft white cotton sleeper. Finally, I wrapped you up tightly in your baby blanket, cuddled you close to me, and you began to nurse.

Then something happened that had never happened before in my entire life. It was as if all time stopped and we were the only two people in the world. You stared at me with such intensity that I was caught off guard. On your face, I saw such sweetness and purity, a look of such goodness and generosity, a look so powerful that I was mesmerized. Your look said: "You're my mommy and I love and trust you completely. Auntie Pearl may have more practice at giving me a bath, but

I'd rather you give me one any day, because you're my mommy and it's you that I want."

The love filled the room, and my heart just soared with this joy I had never known before. I held my breath not wanting to forget any of it. You continued to gaze at me steadily. The look you gave me was arresting. It was as if you were transmitting this energy to me, and there was nothing else in the world for us at that moment. Only each other. Mother and child.

The look on your face changed something inside of me, and from that moment on, I knew we would be so intertwined, that nothing would ever come between us. At that moment, I silently vowed to become the best mommy in the world to you, to love you as unconditionally as you loved me, and to never let you down. Not ever.

Suddenly I knew what was important and what wasn't, what mattered and what didn't and I understood the magnitude of the gift that had been given to me. I was afraid to whisper or move or do anything to break the spell. I just wanted to stay there forever. So I held on tightly, and bathed myself in these waves of love, and in the exquisite and luxurious robe of motherhood.

Max, I love you more than you'll ever know, and I pray that life is always kind to you. Just know that I will always remember the feeling between us in your nursery on that November evening. It was precious and almost holy. And it is a moment I will cherish forever.

Love, Mommy

The Magic Key: Your strength of character gave me the confidence to be the best mother I could ever be. Let it always give you the confidence to be all that you can be and to make all of your dreams come true.

For some mothers, the moment they knew they were a mom happened before they'd even laid eyes on their child:
Laurene: I guess part of this is my Catholic upbringing. Because my pregnancy was difficult and in my face, I felt like a mother when I was pregnant. Because of being sick all the time and having to give myself injections for the diabetes, I was already caring for my child before she was born. I can't remember a crystalline moment afterwards. With Brenna it was almost like now you're outside me instead of inside me, but I was always your mother from the moment you were inside of me.

Similar topics:
- ♥ First diaper change
- ♥ First breastfeed
- ♥ First tooth (or losing the first tooth)
- ♥ First steps
- ♥ First foods
- ♥ First words
- ♥ First accident

Use Your Senses — Use all of your senses when you are writing. This is particularly helpful when you are stuck, or can't fully remember. We write evocatively when we are in touch with the five senses — sight, sound, smell, taste, and feel. So when you begin writing, try thinking of your baby in a sensory way: that delicious smell they had after their bath; the way that warm nuzzle spot felt on their little necks; the sound of their laughter or tears; the sight of what they looked like first thing in the morning or how precious they looked lying in their cribs or beds at night; the taste of nibbling on their little toes and the tips of their noses; the sweet smell of their milky breath; the softness of their skin; the feel of them in your arms; the weight of them as they fall asleep on your chest; their hugs; their smiles; how their whole face crinkles and lights up when they smile. Let your senses guide you.

To further ground your writing and evoke the senses, try picturing your child in the environments they exist in — their nursery, their change table, their crib, their rocking chair, the high chair, the park they played in, their backyard, your bedroom, the kitchen, the bathtub — and use those rooms to help you conjure up the memories and then add the sensory associations to make the writing come to life.

Tales From the Playgound

The Swing

THE BATH STORY COULD BE USED as a moment where you have an epiphany, or you could use it as one of a list of firsts. A list of milestones is a great way to start writing or even get unstuck. There really are some very universal ones, like the birth, first bath, bonding, first solid foods, first major holidays or family outings, weaning from breastfeeding, first words, first steps, first accident. One for sure, is our first trip to the playground.

Do you remember the first time you took your child to a playground? What did they enjoy doing at the park? What are your memories of their first time on the swing, the slide, in the sandbox, or on the teeter-totter? What are your memories of taking your baby to the park? This is a letter you can have a lot of fun with, and make it humorous.

Dear Max,

"Delight" is definitely the word that comes to mind when I think of the first time you ever went on a swing: delight, both yours and mine. You were about eight months old at the time. Like many new mothers, even though I'd never been busier, it seemed, on the other hand, as if we had all the time in the world. I wasn't working full-time and our summer days just stretched out languidly before us. Almost every day after lunch we would go for a stroll in the park as part of our afternoon outing.

But, before we could go anywhere, there were always a bevy of baby preparations to get out of the way. First there was bathing you, changing you, feeding you, dressing you, packing up the diaper bag, changing you again, getting the stroller readied for our big expedition, and then after all that, just getting out the door. That was always a triumph, by the way — just making it down the steps and out onto the sidewalk. When we finally did get outside, I think we were both exhilarated just to be breathing in that fresh air, and for my part, after all that work, I had a great sense of accomplishment. Things change when you're a mother. And small things become huge feats because of the time, energy and focus involved. Anything else that might have happened that day was just a bonus. We were outside — how much better did it get than that?

Until that day we had never really talked to anyone on our little excursions, so I was surprised when a little four-year-old girl approached us. "Can you swing me, miss?" she asked. I looked around to see where her mother was, and saw her nanny.

"You know, dear, I'd love to, but I can't leave my baby alone. He's too little," I responded. Now I know that ostensibly, I could have moved the carriage close enough to the swing and pushed the little girl while watching you at the same time, but I was a new mother. How could I take my eyes off you, even for a second? There was just no way. But there was no way the little girl was letting me off the hook either.

Looking implacable with her little hands on her hips, her feet firmly planted in the sand, she suggested impatiently: "Well, why don't you swing *him?*" She glanced upwards to heaven for guidance. I knew she was not going to take no for an answer. Questions raced through my mind: Why hadn't I been swinging you? Is this something I was supposed to do earlier at six months? Who could remember swinging, in the middle of trying to figure out the essentials, like crawling, moving to solids, and how to get to Gymboree class on time?

It occurred to me that this little girl could be on to something. I mean, you were probably ready. And, at the same time, I was a bit taken aback that it took a four-year-old to point out the obvious. So, trying to regain my composure, I answered somewhat defensively, "Because he's too young. He's just eight months old."

Unimpressed, she answered saucily, "Well, I swang for the first time when I was only four months old." She crossed her arms over her chest challengingly.

"Well, I dunno," I muttered. "He's just a baby. . . ."

Not wanting to waste any more time on trivialities, she took control of the situation. "I'll show you. Just take him out of the stroller."

> Don't Procrastinate! — If you make writing a daily routine, your writing will improve and it will become easier to write. We spend so much time avoiding and delaying the task of writing, but once the wheels are in motion, momentum takes over and the stories will pour out of you and you won't be able to stop writing. The key word here is ACTION, and the best cure for procrastination is to take even one small action step, and then enjoy the exhilarating feeling of having accomplished what you set out to do.

We made our way to the baby swings. Waving her hands this way and that, the little girl showed me how I should lift you into this contraption that, all of a sudden, looked rather daunting. Why hadn't I ever noticed before how complex these baby swings were? They may look straightforward enough at first glance, but if you really examine them closely, a lot of planning has gone into them. Picture this: Dangling about two feet above the ground, the baby swing is almost like a sling. It hangs from four long metal chains connected at each of the corners of the seat. The seat itself is made out of a kind of canvas. There is a metal T-shaped bar which is there to hold the child securely in place and this metal bar moves up and down. Now the saddle itself cradles the baby on three sides and the bar creates the fourth side.

There are four, count them four, spaces where the baby's legs could go. You got it, four potential spots.

Two of the holes face in one direction and two others face in the opposite direction. So far, so good. After much deliberation, I finally bit the bullet and put you in the swing with your little legs in two of the holes, so that your back was resting against the metal bar. I was quite proud of myself. I was about to swing you up into the air when I noticed that your poor little legs were splayed out in what was an obviously unnatural position. As I fumbled, trying to make you more comfortable, the little girl barked, "Not that way, silly, his legs are in backwards." As quickly as I could, I lifted you out of the swing, got you disentangled and turned you around. Now you were facing the bar and no longer bent over in a hang-gliding position. You were ready to fly. And I was ready for bed.

I plunked myself down in the sand in front of you, and got ready to swing you. You might be asking yourself why I sat in front of you. Well, there was a very good reason for this: I would be able to see your face and all of your little expressions and reactions to this new experience, which I wouldn't be able to do in the traditional behind-the-child swinging position, and I didn't want to miss a thing. And in all honesty, I was so exhausted from the stress of the four-year-old dictator that sitting down in the sand was a great break for me, too.

Gently at first, I started to push you. As you began to feel the back-and-forth motion of the swing, your eyes and face lit up. I'll never forget that look on your face. It was one of pure, unadulterated joy and bliss. Then, little chortles and whoops and giggles and tinkling laughter: sounds of pure delight began to emanate from somewhere deep inside of you. Never before had I heard these sounds coming from your little being. You were in a word, ecstatic. I was mesmerized and humbled by your real and genuine delight. It was one of the greatest thrills of my life to witness and I felt so grateful to be there with you that day in the park. If you could have spoken, I know you would have said, "Mommy, this is the most wonderful thing in the world. Why have you kept this from me for so long? This is absolutely incredible!"

Then, I don't know how it happened — or why — but all of a sudden, I found myself singing, "Thwingy, thwingy, thwingy / thwingy, thwingy, thwing (sung to the tune of "I'm the King of the Castle"). I guess I just was so caught up in your enthusiasm and that word just seemed right at the time. As I write this, I realize it sounds a bit silly, but part of being a mother I've come to discover is letting go of false pride.

Motherhood transports you to places you've never been before. And what a place we went to that day. That word "thwingy" just worked. And, the more I sang it, the more you whooped with delight. Honestly, I think if I could have bottled the ecstatic expression on your face, not to mention that look of pure unadulterated joy in your eyes, it would be the most sought-after tonic in the history of civilization.

From that day on, we went to different baby swings in different parks in our neighborhood and others, so that you could enjoy as many swings as possible. It became a big part of our time together. Eventually, Daddy hung a red, yellow and blue swing from an old oak tree in our backyard. It had eighty-nine sailor knots tied lovingly by him so that, God forbid, there was no way you were ever falling out of it.

What was it about swinging that gave you so much delight? I think you loved the fresh air, the breeze in your hair, and the exhilarating feeling of freedom. I think you also thought it was kinda cool that Mommy was making this happen for you, lifting you up in the air and taking you on this joy ride.

My delight and joy certainly came from watching your exhilaration. Your first time on that swing was one of the happiest moments of my life.

Love, Mommy

The Magic Key: Always do what delights you. Do at least one thing that gives you total joy and delight in your life.

Anne: There weren't any baby swings in the park near us. So my daughter was older than usual, maybe she was almost a year old. I took her to visit my aunt, and was really pleased to discover that their park had infant swings. I can even remember playing there as a kid myself, so it was really neat. So on our first daily walk to the park, I was thrilled to be able to take her out of the stroller and guide her legs through those secure holes and give her a gentle push and her face just lit up. She was so excited. She giggled and laughed and I took about twenty-five pictures of it.

Similar topics:

♥   Flying a kite

♥   Playing in the sandbox

♥   Taking the stroller on a walk to the park and all the accoutrements that you need when you go out

♥   Your child making new friends at the park

The Bedtime Routine

FOR SOME PARENTS, BEDTIME is a battlefield; for others, it's the best part of the day, and contains some of their happiest memories of their child's early years. Do you remember your child's bedtime routine? What was their routine when they were little? If you had to describe it to someone else, and teach him or her how to do it, what would you say? If you have older children, how has their routine changed, or is it really the same? Writing about your children's bedtime routine is a great place to start writing love letters to your children.

This letter is an example of how to change things up a bit. Rather than write the letter in the form of a strict "Dear Max," "Love, Mommy" format, I've written it as if I'm having a conversation with his father. Kids love this sort of thing, and it makes them feel like they're eavesdropping on a conversation that happened many years ago.

Dear Max,

I was always the one who put you to sleep, and we had established a very specific routine for how to do so. One night, I had to go out, and your poor daddy was left having to follow my instructions. The following is a scene of what happened that evening:

"Okay. First of all you have to begin in the rocking chair. Place Max gently in your lap so that he's facing out, so he can see the pictures in the books that you're reading to him. I've placed his favorite books right there [I point to a spot on the floor, to the right of the rocking chair]. First of all, you have to read about seven to ten books . . . Yeah, you got it. Seven to ten books. It's the only way it'll work. No matter what, always end with the lullaby and sleeping books, for obvious reasons.

"[Exasperated.] Okaaaay, I'll give you the reasons. Because the jumpy books just stimulate him and the lullaby books always go at the end. And also you have to read them slower and speak more softly with each new book, as he begins to get sleepier and sleepier. Oh yeah, don't forget whatever you do, make sure to read all of them before *Goodnight Moon*. *Goodnight Moon* always has to be last.

"Now, during all of this, please have the bottle nearby, but don't offer it to him, because he'll only take it when he's really into the book you're reading. Have the bottle right near you so he can pick it up himself . . . because he's very independent. He always likes to grasp the bottle himself.

"The moment he's done with the bottle, you have to have the pacifier ready for that moment when he throws the bottle away. It happens very quickly. And you have to nimble. Make a quick exchange with the pacifier, but call it a 'paci'. . . . Don't call it a 'pacifier' because he won't know what you're talking about.

Now, while you're reading, play the children's Mozart tape. That always seems to work. Then just before he goes to sleep, you can change the tape to his favorite lullabies which are on the *Rockabye Lullaby Collection*. He's been listening to that same tape since he was born . . . oh, because he's always liked it. It's the one that resonated with him the most when I tried different lullabies with him. Why do you think? Honey, please try to stay with me on this.

"When you're at this stage, also known as the lullaby portion of the evening, you can turn him to face you and start rubbing his back and patting him gently. If he's still jumping up and down, stand up and pat him while you're slow dancing with him. Hope that at this point, he's resting his head on your shoulder.

"Oh, don't look so discombobulated. It's not that hard. Are you still with me? So, as I was saying, make sure you've given him the short paci. Not the long one with the red-and-yellow Winnie the Pooh on it, 'cause that's not safe for night time. Cover him up with his blankets, and rub his back.

"Oh, I forget to tell you that just before you sit down with him, don't forget to gently dim the lights. But I'm sure you knew that already.

"Did you get all of that, honey?"

Max, Moms all over the world have their own variations on this theme.

But this one was mine. Sleep tight. I love you, and sweet dreams.

Love, Mommy

P.S. When I got home that evening, your room looked like it had been attacked by a tornado. All of your books, toys, and clothes were strewn all over the floor. I found you happily at play in a large box that we'd used in our move. Daddy was on the cot beside you, fast asleep. I can't tell you the rest of the story because it's not suitable for family reading.

The Magic Key: You survived in spite of Daddy. But always remember how important every detail was to me when it came to taking care of precious little you.

You can, of course, write about sleeping in a more traditional way.

Dear Lily,

I always loved putting you to bed because I knew I would see you again at some point in the night. I would rock you in your rocking chair and read books to you and nurse you one last time before bed and then you would fall asleep in my arms and I would transfer you to your crib.

The only problem is that at about six months you would cry, and I would come to your crib and you would gently stroke my cheek, and I was toast. As you looked at me with those gorgeous and long black lashes, I could never resist and would take you into our bed with us. That was my first mistake, because as time went on, you got very smart and when you could talk a few months later, you would just say "Mama" very lovingly as you stroked my cheek, and I couldn't resist. Once you were in your own bed, it was even easier and I would hear the pitter-patter of your little feet coming into our room and I would lift you in between Daddy and me.

You are six years old now and these days you come in a little later in the night, usually at about three in the morning and you take a swig from your water bottle and you climb into bed in between us. I know you should be in your bed, but I just love cuddling with you so much and I know that you won't be doing this forever.

You won't, right honey?

Love, Mommy

The Magic Key: You really melt me and your dad as you'll see in the next story.

Dear Lily,
When you were a baby, sometimes Mommy would ask me to put you to sleep at night. I found this very difficult for me to do, even though it seemed to be very easy for Mommy. I would put you into your crib but invariably you would start to cry and I didn't know what to do. So I would try to roll you over, check your diaper,

give you your pacifier, or rub your tummy. Most of the time this did not work. So I had to figure out a way to do this on my own so I wouldn't have to wake up Mommy.

I decided to put a CD player in your room to play some music, which I hoped would soothe you to sleep. When this didn't work I lifted you up and started to slow dance to the music with you. And this always worked like a charm. While I was dancing with you, I would think of all the things you had ahead of you in your life. And how some day I would be dancing with you at your wedding.

Love, Daddy

The Magic Key: You can always count on Daddy and me to comfort you.

Beverly: Bedtime was always fun when the children were small. Bath time first, let's go. Into the bathroom we would go, they would get undressed and hop into the tub full of bubbles. I would sit and watch them as they frolicked in the tub. After they were all squeaky clean they would get out, dry off and get into their nice, clean jammies. Once in bed I would lie between them and we would read a book. They would take turns picking which book we would read. Then, before the lights would go out, they would ask me to 'tell us about when you were a little girl.' I would then proceed to tell them different things that I did when I was little like they were — family get-togethers, sisters and brother things we did as children. They loved these stories and I loved talking to them about me when I was young. They plan on carrying on the tradition. Even now as they are older they still comment on those nights lying there and listening to the little girl stories.

Sometimes the bedtime story isn't a happy one. But you can still write it out for your child, because inevitably it had a happy ending. If bedtime felt more like war than peace, it might be a great way to let your child know that things weren't always perfect, but you struggled through and still loved them no matter what.

Jen: I 'Ferberized' my daughter when she was six months old. And while it was probably the best thing for her, it was one of the worst experiences of my life. I was determined to teach my daughter to sleep without any crying (on her part *or* mine). Every evening would begin with me nursing her for half an hour at a time, with ten minutes of her sleeping in between before calling me back upstairs, for almost three hours. Then she'd be up again every hour and a half all night long and was cranky all day and never napped. After two months of this, one night my husband stopped me from going upstairs for her fourth feeding. 'Let's let her cry for a bit.' I had done a lot of reading on the Ferber method prior to this — the basic idea is to let them cry, going in and reassuring them every few minutes. It teaches the child to put themselves to sleep, and soon they are sleeping well and feeling a lot better for it. But just my luck: my baby didn't slot into a doctor's categories.

She started crying at 9:00, and by 9:45 I was sobbing on the couch. At 10:45 after going in and reassuring her every ten minutes, she was still going strong, and I was exhausted and feeling like the worst parent on the planet. Shortly after 11:00, there was suddenly silence. I went in to check on her, and there she was, asleep. But it wasn't over. At 1:00 a.m. she started up again, and went until 3:00. Ferber said most babies would cry for forty-five minutes: mine cried for 260. Reluctantly, we continued the method for the next few nights until she was sleeping through the night. It worked, in the end, but at a cost for all of us. Yet, her four-hour fight that fateful night when she was six months old taught me that this was one determined little girl, and no matter what the circumstances were telling her, she was *not* going to give up. That same determination is still her most powerful trait today, and makes her such a wonderful little girl to have.

Similar topics:

- ♥ Getting your baby to sleep through the night
- ♥ Baby on board or baby in the bed with you
- ♥ Sweet dreams and bad dreams and how you comforted them
- ♥ Teddy bears, blankies, pacifiers, and other bedtime comforts
- ♥ Lullabies and bedtime books
- ♥ First babysitters

The Born Traveler

DO YOU REMEMBER THE FIRST time you ventured out away from home? You can really have fun with this story because it's usually very humorous. What was it like the first you went away with your baby? Where did you go? What did you do? Do you remember how much you packed and how travel as you knew it changed forever?

Dear Max,

When you were only two months old, which happened to be during the Christmas holidays, Daddy and I decided to take you to the Deerhurst Inn so we could spend a glorious week together as a family. We dreamed of sleigh rides in the snow, magical evenings by the fireside, making snow angels and snowmen — maybe even skating and cross-country skiing with you in the "Snugli"; all warm and toasty in your little red-and-white snowsuit. The fairy-tale fantasy was lovely. But this holiday taught us a valuable lesson. Every time we plan something to a tee, it inevitably plays out differently. Not worse, not better, just differently. Such was the case with our winter vacation.

You came down with your first cold three days before we left. In a panic, I called your pediatrician, Dr. Goldbach, with a million questions. Mainly what I wanted to know was, would it be safe to be that far from the doctor's office. The resort was a three-hour drive, so I couldn't get to the pediatrician's in the four-and-a-half minutes that I'd done in the past.

"Where are you going exactly?" Dr. Goldbach asked.

"The Deerhurst Inn," I replied.

"Oh? Here's my advice, Judy. Go on your holiday, have a great time, and if you run into any trouble just call room 726. That's where my wife and I will be, too."

I couldn't believe my ears. I was so relieved, I practically cried. And then, with renewed enthusiasm and vigor, I set out to get you packed for your first trip.

Auntie Pearl, who had been visiting, asked in her wry manner, "Where are you going? Alaska? For a year?"

I had packed four of your crocheted blankets, about twenty-two receiving blankets, twelve towels with hoods and matching washcloths, every item of clothing you owned, a huge box full of diapers, your bathtub, your strollers, your infant car seat, two different kinds of "Snuglis," everything that was on your change table and a partridge in a pear tree.

Most importantly, I brought the baby medicine chest, which, in the end, was all we really needed because we *all* ended up with your cold. We spent the entire week in our room bathing you, dressing you, doing the laundry, venturing out only to eat, then all of

> **Start Small** — If an entire letter seems overwhelming, try writing one paragraph per story. In fact, if you were to go through the table of contents in this book and write down all the headlines that apply or strike a chord with you, then just fill in the blanks with 25 words or less, before long you'll be itching to write even more. Make it simple and low-key and chances are lots will become even more available to you.

us collapsing into bed, sick as dogs.

Every night at about two in the morning, I would tap on Daddy's shoulder.

"Is he breathing?" I would ask nervously.

"He's breathing, he's breathing," he would mutter, never opening his eyes.

"I don't believe you, your eyes are shut — go check him."

A few minutes later, I'd tap away on his shoulder again. "Get up and check him. I understand you're a doctor," I'd say.

"Right now, I *need* a doctor," he said. "I thought motherhood would relax you, Judy."

"Just *do* it," I said through clenched teeth, my whole heart gripped with fear. After what seemed like an eternity, I'd hear the verdict.

"He's fine, he's fine," he'd say, his exasperation surfacing ever so slightly. "It's *me* that needs help. This is killing me."

But despite everything, what stands out in my memory is one glorious afternoon at the restaurant Three

Guys and a Stove, a day I'll never forget. We bundled you up in your snowsuit, only to unbundle you the minute we got there.

We found a perfect spot right in front of a beautiful stone fireplace, with a roaring fire, nestled right in the back of the restaurant on the second floor. Daddy suggested, "Let's have a glass of red wine. We're all better now and it will be the first meal we've really been able to enjoy this week".

"Cliff, I'm nursing," I said nervously. "Won't it go right through to the baby?"

"As I said," Cliff smiled with a twinkle in his eye, "let's have that glass of wine."

"Okay," I agreed, secretly delighted, as I was looking forward to spending some time alone with Daddy. "Sure," I replied. "I'll just have a glass to keep you company."

I started nursing you and within ten minutes, you were peacefully and happily asleep in my arms. I gently placed you in your infant car seat in the "Snap and Go" stroller right near the warmth of the fireplace, and covered you up with a blanket. You slept beautifully.

Because you were content, Daddy and I were able to enjoy the most delicious bowl of curried-pumpkin-and-sweet-potato soup, garnished with a few sprigs of cilantro, one of the best soups I've ever had. We were also able to spend two uninterrupted, precious hours together having a romantic meal. This trip hadn't played out exactly as we'd hoped, but we learned how to appreciate the blissful "moments" when they do happen.

In the end, our vacation wasn't the idyllic winter

wonderland we'd imagined, but we still managed to experience an exquisite moment in time that I will always remember.

Love, Mommy

The Magic Key: We do such simple things with our babies, and yet somehow the ordinary becomes extraordinary in their presence. Our time was simple and perfect, mostly because we were together.

This exercise isn't just for moms; you can try it, too, Dad!

Josh:

Dear Maxwell,

Do you remember one of our first surprise trips to Winnipeg? You were just twenty-one months old. You and Daddy were going to surprise Papa Hershey for Father's Day. Mommy stayed home in Toronto because she was expecting your sister Samantha. Mommy packed us lots of food and toys for the airplane trip.

I remember pulling up to Grandma and Papa's house in a stretch limousine and the two of getting out ringing the doorbell. There we stood (you were in my arms); both of us ready to burst with excitement. We were about to share a wonderful moment!

Grandma Lainey came to the door first. She was so happy and so surprised that the tears of joy started to roll down her cheek. She called to Papa Hershey, "You've got a couple of visitors." Papa Hershey came to the door. "Happy Father's Day!" we said. He was so surprised and so happy. All four of us had a group hug and no one wanted to stop squeezing.

For Grandma Lainey and Papa Hershey, it was one thing for them to see me, their son, but it was a whole other event for me to bring their grandson (who lives 2,000 miles away) for a surprise visit on Father's Day. It was you, Maxwell, that made the whole surprise that much more special. You made Grandma and Papa so happy and you made Daddy so proud. I love you.

Love, Daddy

Similar topics:
- ♥ Special outings like going to the zoo, the library, an amusement park
- ♥ Regular outings like going to the car wash, the grocery store, dry cleaner
- ♥ Going on your first family vacation, going to the cottage, first airplane ride, train ride, excursion on the bus or subway
- ♥ Going for a walk with your baby, toddler, or young child

Your First Portrait

MOST OF US NEVER GET around to taking a professional portrait of our babies. We rely on our photographic talent, which is sometimes superior to the professional shots anyway. Did you ever take your baby for a professional photo? What was that experience like? What do you remember about the shots you took yourself?

We always take lots of pictures of our first child. The second child doesn't get as many, and often by the third or fourth, we're lucky if we have a handful of shots. That's just the way it is. We get busy. But pictures are still great for memories, and taking them is as much fun as looking back on them years later. There's also something very cool about photos taken on a family vacation. They become the memory keeper, and are a great tool to use if you want to write about those experiences at a later date.

Dear Max,

We aren't one of these families that does everything on time, when you're supposed to. Some families go to Sears when their child is a few months old for the first portrait, another at six months, a year old and so on. Well, I was always so impressed by the quality of Daddy's candid shots that I never bothered, and life just was too busy and it never seemed to work. But one day, Daddy insisted and we got it together, sort of.

For weeks and months and even years, Daddy begged me to get your portrait taken. "You haven't done it yet," he'd ask every Friday. "What are you waiting for?"

But you know, Max, there was always something. We'd be all geared up to do it on a Monday morning, and then you'd come down with a cold. The next time, we'd practically have you bathed, combed, and ready to go out the door, and you'd bang your head on a corner, and have a huge bump on your forehead, or you had this series of eye infections, where your poor little eye was all red and practically closed. It was uncanny. We just couldn't get you into that studio.

"You passed the ten-month mark," Daddy said, anxiety ridden. "That's the perfect time for a portrait. They're not moving yet, but they're so cute. When are you going to do it, Jude?"

Well, the perfect opportunity finally arose when we were at a silent auction and we won a photo session. There was no turning back now. You were having your picture taken. We made the appointment and the morning of the session, we checked and double-checked. No injuries, no illnesses, no impairments of any kind.

You were ready to make your appearance. I assumed you'd be a star, hamming it up for the studio camera the way you always loved having your photo taken by Daddy. But instead, the moment they sat you in front of the backdrop, you tried running for the door. You became shy and scared, and my heart went out to you. It didn't seem to matter what they did. Every toy they brought out had about as little appeal for you as a tuna sandwich.

Here I thought you'd love getting your picture taken, and I saw a very shy side of you for the first time. It was so uncharacteristic of you that I was caught off-guard, and I didn't have my bag of tricks on hand to distract you and make you more comfortable.

The very patient photographer wouldn't give up. He offered you every toy in the place and did his best *Sesame Street* impressions, but to no avail.

"What do you think would really make him feel comfortable?" he asked. I thought and thought of all your favorite toys and books at home that I wished I brought, like your yellow pull car that sings, or your Walking Talking Elmo or your favorite *Tool Book*. But there was no point, because it was too late to go home now. Then all of a sudden I had a moment of clarity. "Of course! Do you have any Mozart tapes?"

"Mozart?" he said, seeming surprised. "Oh, you mean the composer. Well, gee, uh, would Barney do? I'm sure we've got a Barney tape lying around," he said hopefully.

"That's okay," I said, thinking quickly on my feet. "I'll just hum a few bars of it. It works every time."

So there I stood beside the photographer, and I hummed a few bars of Mozart's fourth Piano Sonata in G Minor. I must have looked whacked as I sang the tune of the familiar song, "Bah . . . bah bah . . . bah bah bah bah bah bah! Bah . . . bah bah . . . bah bah bah bah bah bah! Now strings!" But it worked.

We got our shot.

Love, Mommy

The Magic Key: Max, always keep some Mozart in your treasure chest. You've always loved music, and remember you can always turn to your music whenever you need a lift, comfort, relaxation, fun, and recharging. Stay with your piano and your love for music. You come from a long line of music lovers and music makers. Rock on!

Similar topics:
- ♥ Taking baby photos with your own camera, and some funny stories of what happened
- ♥ What are your child's favorite pictures (and yours!)
- ♥ Poring over family albums
- ♥ Family videos
- ♥ School photos and class pictures
- ♥ Camp photographs

Letters from Both Parents — Involve your partner in the writing process. Not only will this give your child a new perspective of memory, but it will enhance your own relationship, too. The coziest feeling for a child is knowing that their parents loved each other — that can be a huge feeling of reassurance and comfort for them. This allows you to spend time together, reminiscing about how you began your life together. Plan a romantic candlelit dinner. Look into each other's eyes and remember all of the joy and passion and excitement that brought you together in the first place. Then imagine how you would like to tell your children all about how you first became a couple and your early days as newlyweds. Take a tape recorder and talk and have one of you write notes while the other speaks. One of you can type into a computer, while the other talks, then switch. Write two separate letters, and then compare them to see how different your recollections are. Come up with some questions ahead of time.

The First Separation

THE FIRST TIME WE'RE AWAY from our children for any length of time is agony for most parents, because we know it's just the first step away from us, and soon they'll be independent little creatures. Having to drop your child off at a camp or a day care is often one of the first long separations. What was it like with your babies? What was the first day care, camp, or school drop-off experience like? How did you prepare your child for it? How did they react? How did you react? Think back to the steps that led to greater and greater independence for you and your children. Give them details, and name some of the friends they had at the time. It just might jog their own memories.

Dear Max,

We first saw your backyard camp in the winter when the yard was covered with snow. Peeking out from the snow banks were a giant old, abandoned white-and-pale-blue boat, the corner of a swing set, and the tip of a red slide. You couldn't really see much of anything but you were excited nonetheless. And for weeks you went on and on talking about this backyard camp and you would say, "And there's puppets and water play and a sandbox," and you would seem so excited, not even realizing what backyard camp was.

The reason I decided to send you to a camp was because you had never been dropped off in a playgroup or day care program and left without Mommy by your side. So I was concerned that you would be going from zero drop-offs to nursery school in the fall, which was five mornings a week. Someone suggested that this would ease the transition for you and for me and that it would be a really good place to start.

I agonized over the camp for a few weeks and then finally heard about one called Imagination Plus. It was described as a "fun-filled, active summer program that will stimulate your child's imagination in an interactive and creative setting." Daily activities included free play, circle time with songs, games and snacks, arts and crafts, kids sports, story time, and an Imagination Plus activity that included dramatic play, puppetry, memory games, and language development. There were also four teachers for sixteen children. The camp was only three days a week and lunch was not part of the deal. I could actually pick you up and take you home for lunch with me. On a cold day in February, we went down to check out the camp, and the owner of the camp told me her philosophy on separating on the first day of camp: "Look, Judy, if I see that your child is crying, I've been known to pick them up and carry them around for two hours." I decided to sign you up.

July 4, 2000, arrived. I'd been dreading the day for weeks. I was determined to be one of the first moms there, so you would never feel abandoned in any way. Your clothes and shoes had been name-tagged with our indelible black marker. You had your sunscreen, diaper bag, and sun hat. You looked so handsome.

We practiced our line, and I drove you to your camp. When I got there and took you into the backyard, I tried the line again: "Mommy leaves . . ." But this time, you finished my sentence with, "Mommy always comes back, but please stay here with me today, Mommy."

I didn't know what to do. My eyes were welling up with tears, but I was determined not to show them to you. My heart was breaking, but I tried to conceal it from you. I knew it would only make it worse.

I thought quickly on my feet. "Engage them in an activity that they'll enjoy," I had heard. We tried the sandbox, only you wanted me inside there with you. We tried the swings. Nothing doing. We tried some puzzles, usually your favorite, but it didn't work. Finally, I used what the counselor had told me. You always loved a pretty face, so I looked for one and found Celine, one of your counselors. "Would you hold him?" I asked her. "Please just hold him to ease the transition." She was a darling and did just that. I kissed you and said I'd be right back.

Then I got into my car and I wept. I cried all

Those First Funny Words — Parents, a quick way to capture memories is just to write down the words as they say them, because they'll be gone far too quickly if you don't get them down on paper. I called these first precious words Maxisms and Lilyisms, and I still laugh at the sweet memory of them. You will, too. (Warning: Only you, your partner, some family members, and the child will find these exceedingly funny. When you tell other people about them, they'll just smile politely, but not really get it at all. These are "in" jokes for the immediate family, but boy, are they ever hilarious.)

Maxisms: "Brefixt"; "I share wif Lily good"; "I lub ooh Mama"; "Brudder"

Lilyisms: "Dees one"; "Tank ooh"; "Daddy is a booful boy"; "Spahderman" (the cutest)

morning. Pickup was at 11:45, only I showed up at 11:30. I found you in the sandbox, looking so sweet and so exhausted from the heat, the activity, and probably just the newness of it all. My heart went out to you. We were both so relieved to see each other. We'd made it through our first morning of camp. Day two was pretty much the same. All I remember about that day is that sweet, shy, and very woebegone and relieved smile you gave me when I came for you to pick you up. On day three you cried, but you quickly adjusted and really started to like the camp. You had little friends that you talked about — Billy, Robby, and Rachel — and you learned about baseball and football and badminton and boats, and you made some great crafts.

On your last day of backyard camp, I dropped you off for your wrap party. They served ice cream and gave out loot bags, with these really cool sunglasses. You look adorable in them. We kissed the counselors goodbye, said goodbye to the friends you made, and Billy was sad to say goodbye to you and said, "Bye, Max. I'll see you next time." You didn't answer right away, and then very sweetly, you said, "Bye, Billy." I loved the way you said goodbye, and what a good soul you are.

We went out and had chocolate doughnuts and celebrated. We'd laid the foundation for our next project, nursery school in September.

Love, Mommy

The Magic Key: Max, doing new things can often be a little scary. But what's cool is that whenever you do them, they usually work out really well. When I think of hockey camp and how you loved it, trying out the gondola at Tremblant, and so many other moments like that, I know that if you just take a deep breath and jump, it always works out in the end. So don't be afraid to try new things.

Often the first separation isn't when your child leaves you, but when you have to part with the child:

Laurene: Brenna was six months old, just weaned. I was still having some discomfort and fullness. We'd gone cold turkey because she wouldn't take bottles. So neither of us had been particularly happy for the last week of my maternity leave. So as I said, I dropped her off at a home that our agency supervised and I knew in my head it was a good placement for her. And I dropped her off I gave her all the usual instructions and tried not spend too much time, because you want to make it a nonemotional parting. And then I got in my car and the tears started before I was even out of the driveway. I got into the office and mopped myself up as good as I could before I went to my desk. And everybody who came by to welcome me back to work wished they hadn't, because each time it set off the tears again. It seemed like the longest day, and I only allowed myself to call the day care provider once. And of course, everything was fine, but I didn't really believe in it until I picked her up again and saw with my own eyes that she was okay.

Similar topics:
♥ First day care drop-off
♥ First day at school
♥ First sleepover
♥ First time at day camp
♥ First time at overnight camp

Developmental Milestones

Bye-Bye, Pacifier

WE REALLY DO FEEL WHAT OUR babies feel, sometimes even more than they do. Think back to the first time your child really had to give up nursing, or a bottle, their pacifier or their nap. Or what about their baby blankie, or a favorite book or stuffed animal? How did your baby react? How did you react? What was it like during the process of having to give up that "something" that was so dear to them? And what did you do when victory was achieved?

Dear Max,
Strength of character is something you've always had. The best example of this was how you gave up your pacifier, something you loved right up to when you were three years old. It wasn't an easy thing to do and you handled it with dignity, grace, and aplomb.

The paci was a member of our family from the first

time we gave it to you when you were a newborn. I didn't realize then that that little white-and-blue object would become the centre of your universe.

Maybe it was all my fault. It wasn't as if I hadn't been warned. I mean, Auntie Marcy told me that she always got rid of the soother when her babies were three months old, period. I, on the other hand, let you have yours for three years.

That isn't to say it didn't have its usefulness. It was a good friend to you. It came in handy in restaurants to soothe you to sleep so that Mommy and Daddy could go out and take you with us. It also helped you during our many takeoffs and landings when we flew.

You had your own particular adorable style for using your paci, too. You would flip up the little white handle so it rested just under your nose, which seemed to make you feel really warm and secure. Had a talent scout been looking for a poster boy for pacis, you would have been it.

But eventually Mommy and Daddy realized that you couldn't use it all day, every day. So we decided to isolate its use for naptime and bedtime. That first separation from your closest friend was a hard one. Being very intelligent, you quickly found a way around this restriction: you started to say you were sleepy long before you really were, just so you could have your paci. I usually gave in, even though I knew it was only going to make it harder for you when you had to give it up for good.

On the first weekend in January of the New Year, you were three years and two months old, the time had

Become a Reporter — Interview the kids at various ages. I remember interviewing Lily at four years old, both on tape and by having her talk while I typed her words out on the computer. It is so wonderful to hear how she expressed herself at four years old and beyond. I also have always put my children's voices on our answering machine as one- and two-year-olds, and we never tire of hearing the sounds of babyhood even as they get older. You can also interview them as a pre-schooler, at age six and seven, then again at nine and ten, and at fourteen, and show how the questions and their answers would change each time.

come. We had the whole weekend together without the hectic routine of the week to interfere.

I was ready. I'd read tons about how to help you stop using the pacifier and even consulted your pediatrician. He made a great suggestion: Go to a shopping mall and, in a kind of ritual, throw out all the pacis into a garbage can, far away from home. To celebrate our liberation, we should then go and buy a special present. But when the time came, I knew that ultimately, we had to find our own way.

I made a plan. I started by reading the book *Bye-Bye, Pacifier* to you for weeks. Then I threw out all the pacis in the New Year. I decided to create my own Quit Paci Program, with its own twelve steps. I told you that tonight you were going to sleep without a paci for the first time. Around 10:30 p.m. which was on the late side for you (9:30 being your usual bedtime), we went up to your room with your blue sippy cup filled with warm milk.

When you realized that there was no paci, you began bargaining. Then you looked everywhere in the hope that there was one I missed.

You were becoming frightened. You started to beg me for a paci, any paci. You even asked if you could use the thermometer paci to take your temperature. I told you that we hadn't used that one since you were a little baby and I didn't know where it was.

You started to cry. It wasn't the crying of a little boy who wasn't getting something he wanted; it was the mournful, painful, sad, and fearful crying of someone who realizes they have to part with something, something that has given them great comfort and security. It hurt me so much to hear you cry like that.

Things were looking pretty desperate. Then I had a brainstorm. I enlisted the help of Teddy (your favorite grey teddy bear). Pretending that he was whispering to me, I told some jokes. Then I told you he had a message for you: "Just a minute, Max, Teddy is saying something." I told you Teddy said he "wanted Max to hug him." Do know what you said, Max? You said, "Mommy, I know why Teddy is saying that."

"Why?" I asked.

"Because he's scared."

"Why do you think he is scared?"

And, Max, you said, "Because he has no paci anymore."

I quickly responded by saying, "Well, Teddy is going

to keep you company all night, just like the paci used to." You found this very comforting.

Then, to distract you, I promised to read as many books as you wanted until you were ready for sleep. So we read *Bye-Bye, Pacifier,* then *Bye-Bye, Bottle*. Then I read you the entire anthology of the *Winnie the Pooh* stories, about two hundred pages. This took several hours, and finally I saw your eyes getting heavy, your eyelids fluttering, and you were getting really sleepy. I patted your back and held you until you fell fast asleep. You woke up a few times in the middle of the night, and once you even said, so forlornly, "Mommy, I lost something. Can you find it?" Each time I rocked you back to sleep.

When you finally did wake up, the first thing you said was, "I have no more paci now." I hugged you and kissed you and told you how proud I was of you. And I promised you we would buy something special to celebrate your first night without a paci.

When Daddy woke up he hugged you, too, and told you how proud he was of you. We called so many people and they told us how proud they were of you because as anyone who knew you really well knew that the paci was a big part of your life.

Later that day, you made it through naptime with no paci. You achieved one of the hardest milestones of your little life and you did it with courage. You did it bravely and sweetly and full of grace. I'd never been prouder of you. Congratulations, Max!

Love, Mommy

The Magic Key: When you were really sobbing, I said to you: "Let me be your paci." What I meant by that is that I will always be there for you. Whenever you need that from me, know that it's there. And I know that one day, you'll learn how to be your own paci, how to soothe and calm yourself down when necessary. I think you're already on your way, and you're only three. You gave something up that you really loved because it wasn't good for you anymore. You're terrific! We're so proud of you!

Rather than use this letter as a story about something ending, you could write about something else they were attached to, but didn't have to give up (unless it fell apart):
Sharon: Adam, when you were four years old, you had a favorite pillow, that you called Piyo because you had a hard time pronouncing your l's. You found your Piyo in my bedroom, on my chaise lounge, and I let you have it because it made you so happy. It had the same material as my bedspread and it had a very soft trim around it that you loved to caress. After a hard day at preschool, you would come home and ask, 'Where's my Piyo?' You took Piyo with you everywhere around the house. While you were eating, playing, watching TV, and of course, sleeping. There were times when you didn't want to go somewhere, like swimming lessons, or something, so you would plant yourself down in the hallway and pout. Then, you would lift your head up, flash your ocean-blue eyes at me and ask 'Piyo in the

car?' Of course, I would say yes and you would jump into the car with me.

Similar topics:
- ♥ Giving up nursing
- ♥ Weaning from breastfeeding or bottle
- ♥ Moving to a grown-up cup
- ♥ Eating habits
- ♥ Diapers and pull-ups
- ♥ The potty

Celebrations

The Birthday Party

WHAT DID YOU DO FOR YOUR child's first birthday? Did you make a party with family and friends? Do you remember the cake? Was there a moment that stands out that you'll never forget? Write to your child about their first birthday or any birthday party that was particularly memorable.

Dear Lily,
Around the time I was making preparations for your second birthday, you had this love for *Mary Poppins*. You watched the movie constantly and would walk around the house saying, "I love *Mary Poppins*" and "Poppins" was said with this slightly nasal quality that made it even more endearing, making it sound like "tuppins." But, Lily, for some time, Mary Poppins was all you wanted twenty-four hours a day. So whenever Julie Andrews, or Mary as you preferred to call her,

descended from the sky with her umbrella with the parrot perched on top and her carpetbag, your whole face would light up and you'd laugh this infectious laugh that would make everyone laugh right along with you, because of the innocent glee and joy that you were feeling.

I don't think I've ever found you as adorable as when you discovered your love for *Mary Poppins*. We had always watched the movie as I, too, have always had an affinity for it. Max watched the movie for a while, too, but then tired of it, and moved on to *Shrek*, *Batman*, *Tarzan*, *Hercules* and *The NeverEnding Story*. But you, Lily, once you got hooked to *Mary Poppins* you wouldn't consider anything else. It had to be Poppins and as often as possible.

So when it came time for your second birthday, I knew I had to make a Mary Poppins birthday party for you. There could be no other alternative.

But there was one problem: Mary Poppins tableware or anything with Mary Poppins on it didn't exist, because in the '70s they didn't have the kind of merchandising they do now. So how to find Mary Poppins for my little Poppins girl who never asked for anything and to whom I just wanted to give the world?

So I took a picture of Mary Poppins from the cover of the videotape and scanned it on the computer and added the words: "Starring Julie Andrews, Dick Van Dyke, and featuring little Lily Librach." Then I brought it to a printing house that specializes in wedding invitations and I asked them to make me thirty colored eleven-by-seventeen placemats which were then laminated.

I did the same thing with the invitations and then found purple, red, and yellow plastic tablecloths to match the placemats, and I rented cute little white plastic tables and children's chairs and made a long table out of all of them, which we were able to decorate with all of the colorful placemats, plates, and cups.

Then I got balloons in all the pretty reds and purples, whites and yellows and we even had a real live Mary Poppins make an appearance. We had a couple of rehearsals over the phone with Marcy, one of my oldest friends, who was pretending to be Mary Poppins. Marcy was a children's musical theater performer. One day she put on a British accent and called you, and said, "Hello, Lily. It's Mary Poppins," and you shook your head, pushed the phone away, saying, "No more this one."

I said, "Marcy, you're going to have to bone up for the real party." Marcy replied, "This is too much pressure. I don't have this much aggravation when I do a real gig."

We were going to hoist Marcy up to the top floor and lower her down like Mary Poppins, descending from the sky, but alas, Marcy would have no part of it, and neither would the many guys we had enlisted to lift and lower her down from the second floor.

I had an old hat, and we had an old wooden coat and hat rack, which I painted white for the occasion. And so we hung the black hat with little red poppies and daisies on it to represent Mary Poppins's hat. Then we hung the carpet bag on one of the hooks and adorned the rest of the rack with red ribbons, balloons and a giant red bow. It looked terrific.

Here are Auntie Marcy's recollections of your second birthday party: "She was awestruck when she saw me and in wonder that this character was there. She sat with me on the stairs and we sang all of the songs together and then twirled our white lace umbrellas (part of your loot bags) and danced together."

The best part of your party, Lily, is that you were enchanted, and I really felt that I was making your dream come to life. To this day, you have a special place in your heart for both Mary Poppins and Auntie Marcy.

Love, Mommy

The Magic Key: It was fabulous that you loved Mary Poppins for as long as you did. And your loyalty to that film and the character was lovely to see. Also I have always loved teaching you and your brother how to celebrate life and to enjoy life's celebrations to the fullest and we've always done that really well.

Maybe the party wasn't the perfect day you imagined, and at the time it seemed devastating. But often those stories are the funniest. Years later, of course:

Laurene: When Jamie turned five, we had just moved into a new house and we were watching our money pretty carefully. We decided to have a low-key birthday party. And he was able to invite a few friends over, maybe five, because I always went with the one friend per each year of the child's age birthday rule of thumb, and so it made sense that for his fifth birthday, he could have five friends. He decided he wanted a Batman cake and I was making the cake for him. So we picked up Batman napkins and cups and I looked around and found a Batman figurine that I thought I could place on top of the Batman cake. We got to the cake and I was trying to make Batman-blue icing. It came out more swimming-pool blue and when I put Batman on top of the cake, he promptly sank up to the top of his knees and then looked like Batman wading through a swimming pool. Try as I might, we couldn't get Batman up and it was like he was sinking in quicksand. We just presented the cake to Jamie as it was and he just looked at it and said, 'What is Batman doing? This isn't the kind of cake I wanted.' We just laughed. Sometimes it just doesn't go the way you planned. The reality didn't live up the vision. But every time we tell the story, we all have a good laugh and now we order ice-cream cakes with someone else doing the artwork.

Similar topics:
You can use these same guidelines to write about any special holiday or celebration that involved your child.
♥   Christmas or Chanukah stories
♥   Mother's or Father's Day celebrations
♥   Favorite Halloween dress-up stories

> ## Remembering Birthdays Past — Jot down
> some highlights that you remember from each
> birthday or a composite of all the birthdays until five
> years old. Just write down some headlines, like "Your
> Second Birthday," and fill in the blanks later when you
> have the time. Try to remember what the theme was,
> where the party was held, what the loot bags or party
> favors were, what refreshments you served, what kind
> of cake you had, the highlights from the party. Did your
> child receive a special gift that they loved? Did they
> have a great time? Is there one special moment,
> person, or place that stands out for them in one of
> their parties? Which birthday was the happiest and
> most memorable for your child? Is there a memory that
> was happiest for you?

Here's an example of a Christmas story by a mother with twin girls.

Maureen:

Dear Sarah and Isabella,

For your first Christmas you were only a few months old and we all slept through the entire Christmas. We were all so sleep deprived that even though we had a tree, we kind of missed the Christmas boat. For your second Christmas, you were more excited about the boxes, the wrapping paper, and the pretty ribbons than you were about all the presents. You couldn't care less about the presents. I remember we got both of you your very own doll strollers, one for each of you. But you guys preferred pushing the boxes around that they came in, rather than the strollers. And no matter how many times we would tell you, "This is the present, play with this," you would look and then go right back to playing with the boxes again. For your third Christmas, you finally got it and mostly what I remember about that was your excitement about everything. I bought you each a calendar and you could open a window every day to count down the days to Christmas. Putting up the lights was exciting, the Christmas tree was thrilling, everything was such a joy to you and it brought us back to believing in Christmas again, because we saw it through your eyes.

Special Outings

The Nutcracker

DO YOU REMEMBER THE FIRST time you took your child to a play or a ballet, or a concert or movie? How did they respond? What was it like? What was it like for you to watch them? Try to recreate the moment for them, as if they were right back in the same seat, watching it all over again.

Dear Lily,

I had seen the production *The Nutcracker* at Christmastime, practically every year since I arrived in Toronto at nineteen years old. When I mentioned that I was taking my daughter to the ballet, I remember a couple of people were shocked. "Why would you take a nine-month-old baby to the ballet, what are you thinking?" But I was determined. I'd been playing music to you and Max since before either of you were even born. So it made sense that if listening to music in utero, as all the books

Notice the Little Things — Instead of praising our children for what they do or what they accomplish, I really believe that we have to notice them, acknowledge them, value and affirm and respect them for who they are. It all begins with noticing who these people are and describing for them what you see that makes them special and unique. Here is where you can really look into their hearts and their souls and share with them your observations of them as these precious and magical beings. Think of the Magic Keys as pearls of wisdom for your children. If your child took all of them — praise about their patience, calm, generosity, sweetness, strength, animated smiles, contagious laughs — and strung them all together, they would have a charm bracelet or necklace that would be a constant reminder of their best traits, characteristics, or special gifts.

say, is beneficial for a baby, the chance to hear a live, sixty-piece orchestra play Tchaikovsky's *The Nutcracker*, would be even more stimulating and exciting for you. And you would be seeing some of the best dancers in the world bring the tale to life. Who knows? I thought. Maybe someday, you'd be up there with them.

The morning was spent dressing you for the ballet. You wore a pretty pink dress with a black velvet bodice, a cotton-candy-pink skirt with a pretty sash, also in the velvet, around the waist that we tied into a bow; perfect for the ballet. Underneath the skirt were layers of ballet-pink crinoline and pink tights, the same color as your dress. On your head, you wore a white lace headband and a matching white lacy sweater. Your golden hair was brushed until it shone. You looked just like a little ballerina yourself.

From the moment the overture began, you began to sway to the music, gently, back and forth. Your whole "self" lit up and came alive with your enjoyment of the ballet. Your happy, open smile never left your face. It was so infectious, we had to smile, too. Toward the end of the first act though, you started to rub your eyes. So you and I quietly retreated to the back of the theater so we wouldn't disturb anyone in case you started to cry. There I rocked you to sleep in my arms at the back of the house, as we watched the lighting guys follow the dancers and light the ballet. When you were fast asleep, we returned to our seats. Your timing was impeccable. You slept through intermission but woke up just in time for the second half of the program. You were thankfully awake for the Sugar Plum Fairy scene. You watched, captivated, as the fairy stepped out of her home inside a beautiful Fabergé egg at the center of a golden palace, never taking your eyes off her as she descended from her majestic throne. You watched with rapt attention right until the end of the ballet. I watched you, imagining what it must be like for you to see this spectacle. I was so glad I'd brought you, especially during the finale.

The stage was alive with snowflakes, lambs, children, flowers, branches, the Nutcracker, the Snow Queen, her icicles, the Sugar Plum Fairy, the children Marie and Misha, the waiters, bees, dogs, cats, mice, goats, roosters, horses, unicorns, and snow maidens, everyone from the land of snow and of the Sugar Plum Fairy — an enchanted land of make-believe coming to life before your eyes.

As a keepsake, we got you a pink stocking in the shape of a ballet toe shoe complete with long satin ribbons, and Max got a miniature Nutcracker marionette at the boutique inside the theatre.

Lily, I'd seen the Nutcracker over a dozen times before that day, but sitting in the theater, watching your face come alive with wonder, it was like I was watching it for the very first time.

Love, Mommy

The Magic Key: This auspicious beginning led to your love of ballet. From the tender age of three, you started taking ballet lessons, and this is your fourth year of studying classical ballet. You love it and the dance form loves you right back. You are made for ballet. Your gracefulness, athleticism, delicate frame, poise, carriage, and "that face," as Grandma Jean calls you, makes you a natural. But most of all, you love it and you shine when you are dancing!

Similar topics:
♥ First play or musical
♥ Going to a children's concert
♥ First movie in a movie theatre
♥ Going to a baseball, football, basketball, or hockey game

Spirited or Spiritual?

Your Child's Inner Beauty

WHEN DID YOU NOTICE YOUR child in awe of something? When did you watch your child become aware there was something more than them, and that they were a part of something bigger? It might have been when they saw a rainbow for the first time, or a sunset, or stars in the sky. It might have been when they looked at a flower, or a tree, or an animal. Maybe it was on a nature walk, at a cottage, on a lake, or camping where they showed a sense of kinship with nature. Or maybe they were inside a church or synagogue. What about the time they said something that revealed how spiritual they were? Maybe they saw a painting or listened to some music that rendered them speechless. It's in these moments that we discover our child's inner spirituality. What are the moments where your child's spirituality revealed itself?

Dear Max,

You had just turned three, and you were one of the youngest in your class at Holy Blossom Nursery School. Every afternoon when I picked you up at school you would run down the hallway past the exit to leave the school and into the Holy Blossom Temple Sanctuary. You would sit down in the front row and I would sit beside you and you would say, "It's so peaceful here. It's so quiet."

We would sit like that for a while, and then I'd carry you around to look at all the stained-glass windows and all the stories and holidays they represented. Then you would say, "Lift me up," and I would let you pick out a keepah and you would wear it, and then look at the Torah and comment on it in hushed, revered tones, like you understood already that the Torah was something very holy. And then the caretaker would clear his throat, and we would nod and start making our way to the parking lot and to our car.

There was something about that place that made you feel safe and secure, and maybe more, who knows. The other day when I asked you what you wanted to be when you grow up, you answered, "A healer."

And I said, "Oh, you mean, a doctor, like Daddy."

And you said, "No, I mean a healer."

And I asked you what that meant, and you said, "I want to heal people from the inside."

You weren't just saying these words: you are a spiritual healer already, and don't even know it. Here's an example: You and Grandpa Siblin both share a love for hockey and for the hockey player Sidney Crosby. Grandpa once asked if you had a Sidney Crosby hockey card, because he was really interested in seeing it. For months you tried to get that card, and finally traded many cards just to get one Sidney Crosby in return. You were so excited to put it in your blue binder with all of your other hockey cards and show it to Grandpa the next time we went to Montreal. In the meantime, Grandpa became very ill and you asked me if I thought it would help if you gave him that very valuable Sidney Crosby hockey card. For you, that card was your most prized possession, but you decided to give it to Grandpa to make him feel better. And he did get better. I think that in some way you believed that the hockey card is what healed Grandpa. But really, Max, it was you.

If you're ever wondering what really resonates with you one day, and what you want to be when you grow up, maybe part of the answer is in this story.

Love, Mommy

The Magic Key: You have a gift of being compassionate, just like your Daddy. I hope you always find joy in reaching out to others. And also, remember to always take the time to be quiet and at peace before the things that awe you. Then hold them deep inside for the times in your busy life when you will need them, so that you can relax and feel that sense of calm in the storm. Max, having a moment in your day where you stop and breathe, meditate, pray, or just be calm and serene is the best gift you can give yourself and those around you.

Your Wider Circle of Love — This a great exercise that I have used in all of my workshops. I suggest to parents that they create little Love Notes (I used lavender stationery folded into four), and hand them out to people in your child's life, like a caregiver, nanny, coach, teacher, grandparent, other parent, best friend, anyone who knows the child well and ask them to write an anecdote that best describes your child. Or ask them to describe your child in twenty-five words or less or to describe a wonderful moment they shared with your child. As well, you can write about loving people in your child's life and tell your child all about the impact these people had on you.

Ask the people you interview:

- Describe my child in a paragraph or less.
- Tell one or two of your favorite anecdotes about the child, a special moment or happening or experience that you shared or witnessed with the child.
- What words of advice or wisdom would you like to impart to them?

Similar topics:

♥   What do you remember about hugs and cuddles with your child

♥   Loving moments

Grace Under Pressure

The Ballet Recital

I DECIDED TO USE THIS LETTER to tell Lily about something that had happened at one of her classes, and how proud I was of the way she handled it. You can combine sentiments in one letter; maybe the child already remembers the extracurricular activities they did, or you want them to remember it, but can't think of a way to tell the story without it sounding like you're just recounting the events of that activity. Add something to the story that is touching or funny, one anecdote (or as many as you'd like) that broadens the scope of the letter. It's a great way to again remind them of the people they were when they were small, through their actions and reactions to the people, places, and things in their lives.

Dear Lily,
You had been taking ballet lessons for two years when it was time to be a part of a serious ballet production:

a performance of *Snow White*, directed by your ballet teacher. Daddy and I were so proud of you, and had been telling everyone about how talented you were as a ballerina.

I bought you pink roses in cellophane and you were the most beautiful Snow White I'd ever seen. In the car, on the way to the performance, you kept saying, "Daddy's coming too, right, Mommy?" And naturally, I assured you that, of course, he would be coming. But I was worried. I called the hospital, and found out that Daddy was running a little late. But I reassured myself that he would arrive on time, and busied myself with getting you ready, securing our programs and our seats, and tucking the flowers underneath my chair. Daddy unfortunately had an emergency at the hospital, and I begged the ballet mistress to hold off the performance for another few minutes, hoping he would arrive in time. But finally, she couldn't hold up things any longer, and the show had to begin.

You were already behind the black velvet curtain, and I was so frantic that you would notice the empty seat beside me. The curtains opened, the performance began, and Daddy still wasn't there. I relaxed for a while when I saw that you were concentrating so much on your little steps and pliés and on the choreography, comforting myself with the fact that you hadn't noticed a thing. The performance was flawless (said the unbiased mother), and the audience was wildly applauding.

And then it happened. The teacher stood up and said, "Would all the fathers of all the twelve Snow Whites please rise and come and dance with your daughters?" My heart started beating wildly in a total panic. I didn't know what to do. All the fathers were getting out of their seats and making their way down the aisle to greet their little girls.

Your eyes found mine. I'll never forget the look in them. You looked scared, like a deer caught in the headlights. Your eyes were wide and vulnerable and I realized that despite me thinking you hadn't noticed Daddy's absence, you had. That's when I also realized that maybe Daddy wasn't there, but *I* was. I somehow rose out of my seat, put on my brightest smile, and walked over to you. I held you in my arms, and lifted you up to me, and danced with you cheek to cheek. I kept telling you over and over again how proud I was of you, how beautiful you were, and how much I loved you. I've never loved you more than at that moment.

You looked sad, but you didn't make a sound; you looked fragile, but you maintained your dignity. You just never left my cheek and you held me more tightly than you ever had before. It hurt so much to see your pain and in that moment, I realized, despite my best efforts, I would not always be able to protect you. And that hurt even more.

But somehow together we got through it, and everyone started to leave and finally Daddy arrived. I asked the accompanist if she could play "Someday my Prince Will Come" one more time so that you and Daddy could dance together. The accompanist agreed, but you shook your head. You knew that the moment was gone and couldn't be recaptured.

Doctors' wives all over the world know how I felt at

that moment, but this is the sacrifice of being married to someone who creates miracles for people every day. As much as I was hurting, I knew Daddy was hurting even more, and he would make it up to you somehow. He took you out for ice cream and bought you a doll to congratulate you. He never missed another one of your performances, and I can tell you that he adores you beyond compare. He is so proud of you and often tells me he can't wait to dance with you at your wedding one day.

This is life and everything doesn't always go perfectly. It's how we find happiness in all situations and how we show grace under pressure that counts. And you, even more than I, did a superb job of it that day. You're our star and my inspiration.

I love you.

Love, Mommy

The Magic Key: Always show grace under pressure, Lily, and, sweetheart, I think you have a natural ability for doing just that.

The Year in Headlines — So many people talk about how they could kick themselves for not writing. A great way to write is sometimes just to make headlines of the top stories that happened that year. Do it on their birthday, and list five of the top things that happened, like their ballet recital or winning baseball game, their birthday, first day of school, best friend, and holiday celebration. Then fill in the blanks. How do you know when you have to tell a story? When one story keeps popping up into your memory over and over again and it is bothering you that you're not writing it, just jot down a few thoughts and recollections about that memory and at least you will have a chronicling of the event.

Similar topics:

♥ A playdate, program, or activity that brought out the best in your child

♥ The first time your child caught a baseball, their first touchdown, goal, etc.

♥ How your child shone on stage in their dance, music recital, or play

♥ Going to Career Day at your child's school, or bringing them to work with you

How You Started Loving Books

DOES YOUR CHILD LOVE BOOKS? What was his or her first favorite book? What are their favorite books now? What are your memories of reading to your baby and/or your toddler? If your child is not a book lover, this letter could be about anything they're interested in — dolls, cars, train sets, baseball — anything they maybe weren't interested in at first, but developed a deep love for later.

Dear Lily,

When you were really little and I used to read to you, you couldn't sit still. You would slide off my lap and jump and play and run and do anything but sit and listen to whatever I was reading. I was so taken aback the first time you leaped off my lap not wanting to read. I was really surprised. The second time I panicked. What if you really didn't like reading? Reading was the

The Little Things — It's not always the big events that we remember, but the little daily things that made us smile along the way. Make lists of some of your favorite things. If you have a daughter, hairstyles can become one of your favorite things about her. Here is a list of my top ten favorite Lily hairstyles:

1. The headband worn across forehead "hippie style" (but on you, of course, feminine and dainty).

2. The headband worn on top of your head in the classic style.

3. One little umbrella-like "Pebbles" ponytail on top of your head.

4. Two little pigtails lifted up from either side and fastened with a covered elastic.

5. Long hair half down and half up in elastic or what we refer to as a clippy.

6. A French Braid in three sections and tied with elastics and clips, with the rest of your hair hanging down. This was always your signature style.

7. The J. Lo look with one high ponytail fastened with a sparkly elastic, and the rest of your mane long and pretty.

8. Hair lifted up on one side only and fastened with barrettes or clips.

9. The high ponytail or the low ponytail.

10. Au naturel, no clips or barrettes. What a concept!

You could also list their top ten TV shows, videos or movies, outfits, colors, books or foods. The possibilities are endless.

most delicious pastime. What if you didn't like books?

A friend of mine suggested that if I sat on the floor and read one of your board books out loud to the wall, that eventually you would venture over. Laurel said, "Just keep at it, because Lily has to love reading and she will one day." So I stuck with it, reading *Polar Bear, Polar Bear* to the walls and to all of your dolls and stuffed animals, and I tried to do it with expression in order to make it exciting for you. So I would talk softly and then pause for dramatic effect and eventually you ventured over, and you pointed to your favorite page and said, "Ilon, Ilon, what do you hear," mixing up the first two letters of Lion, and I never had the heart to correct you, because it was so cute. And suddenly you were there, and you looked at a few pages and didn't play with the book and climb over the chair, but you sat attentively on my lap and listened. At this point, you would still turn the pages faster than I could read them, but I would gently stop you and say, "Let's just finish this page."

You would position yourself on my lap ready to devour any and all of the books I was reading that evening. Our favorite reading spots were in your rocking chair and later in my bedroom where I had a stack of your books next to my magazine rack, and you would jump off the bed, collect more of your favorites, climb back, or say, "Up, Mommy, up you go," and I'd lift you up and we'd snuggle together, our heads propped up on all the white square-shaped pillows and standard pillows and heart-shaped, round, and rectangular throw pillows, and we'd read together.

You had the most beautiful books given to you when you were born. And the ones you didn't have, I supplemented for you, adding to your collection, until you had a veritable little girl's treasured library of board books, the classics, fairy tales, and some special books that caught my eye, like the *Anne of Green Gables* collection, *The Secret Garden*, some ballet books, and a book called *Into My Mother's Arms*, which was one of our favorites.

A number of people bought you copies of *Lilly's Purple Plastic Purse* when you born. Someone even bought you the matching little dolly with a real little purple plastic purse draped over her arm. There were also all the favorites that Max had always enjoyed, like *Goodnight Moon*; *Mama, Do You Love Me?*; *Polar Bear, Polar Bear*; *The Runaway Bunny*; and one of Max's all-time favorites, *The Very Hungry Caterpillar*.

But I knew that you really loved reading and were totally hooked when I found you one day on the kitchen floor surrounded by books from the white bookshelf that had been my bookcase when I was a little girl. And there you were sitting in that ballet position on your knees surrounded by all these books, and were trying to read. You were actually turning the pages and trying to say what you thought was on each page. It was fabulous to watch. You would chatter away to yourself, as happy as a lark. You were so happy to just entertain yourself. What a treat to see you like this.

I always loved reading to you and now our favorite place is definitely in Mommy and Daddy's white bedroom. We snuggle together and you reach down and pull out your top picks from a beloved selection, and you carry the books and then I carry you into the bed and we cuddle, read, and then say our prayers and cuddle some more, and finally you go to sleep in your mother's arms, just like in the book.

Love, Mommy

The Magic Key: Never give up. Always give something a chance and it could turn out to be something fun, exciting, or even just useful in your life.

Your First Best Friend

I REMEMBER GOING TO A wedding and the groom talking about his first day in grade one, and how his mother said to him, "Just make one friend, a good one, and you'll be set for life." And this little boy walked up to the first kid he liked and said, "Will you be my friend?" Well, thirty years later, this friend, who now lived far away, was the best man at this guy's wedding.

Who was the first best friend your child really connected with? What new qualities did you notice in your child when they played with their friends? What are your memories of your child's first best friend?

Dear Max,

When you were almost three years old, you went to nursery school. You were very shy in the beginning, and it took you a few weeks before you started to get comfortable. But very early on, you met a little boy named

Harrison. His smile was so luminous it would light up the whole room, and you both had a lot in common and just seemed to gravitate to each other. You were born exactly two weeks apart. As the year went on, you started having playdates with Harrison every Monday afternoon and you would play happily for hours together, often having lunch first and then running, climbing, jumping, playing with Harrison's elaborate Thomas the Train collection, and just having fun together.

When the summer after nursery school began, the friendship continued and you played every Monday afternoon and then you were in a playgroup with four

- In *Writing Articles From the Heart*, author Marjorie Holmes suggests using numbered lists as a way to organize and summarize your thoughts. For instance, in my letter about giving Max his first bath, I would write:

   1. I was scared
   2. I was alone when I did it the first time
   3. I wrapped him in his towel with the little hood
   4. I applied moisturizers and powders and I remember the diapers I used
   5. I nursed him, and he slept in my arms peacefully

Then I take that information and write my letter.

- At the beginning of each letter, under the title, write the name of a song that provides the perfect soundtrack to the letter. The songs can be ones that pick up on the content of the letter in some way, or ones that your baby listened to on a tape or CD, or ones that were popular during the times you are remembering.

other little boys. You and Harrison first went to Hillcrest Camp together when you were three years old. Considering that neither of you had a sibling at the time, you guys really were just that to each other.

When camp was over at noon, once a week your little playgroup would spend the afternoon together, at a different boy's house each week, and you'd have lunch together, swim in the wading pool, play outside, run around, have treats, and just have a fabulous time.

You learned how to share with Harrison and definitely it was the first time I saw you really begin to care for a human being and display ongoing compassion, empathy and generosity. Harrison has a condition called Hirschsprung's disease. He was born without the cells necessary to propel food downwards, to digest his food properly. Hence, he had to get the bad part of his digestive tract removed. He's had numerous surgeries in his young life, and also has had related colitis, which he has to live with every day.

Max, you have always helped him, have never teased him, and when he's not feeling well, you would just hang out with him and make him feel better. During the summer after nursery school, when Harrison had to have a procedure and wasn't feeling well, when I told you about it, you started to cry, and you said, "That makes me feel really sad, Mommy." It was wonderful to watch this friendship blossom and take on new levels, and to see how both of you flourished with confidence and pride at what you had both created.

When junior kindergarten started, it would be the first time you weren't in school together. But because you both wanted to, we made sure that you could continue to see each other. We invited him over every Tuesday at four for a playdate and dinner, and then every other week we would go to his house for the same.

You shared the things you loved the best together. You developed a love of trains, and Harrison had fun playing all of your favorite games, like your toy car wash with all the little cars and your toolkit with the "adjustable wench," as you used to put it.

Together, you and Harrison learned how to play hockey, baseball, soccer, football, and basketball. You learned how to swim together, you studied karate together, and even used to run together. And now, because of all of those times together, you are a very strong swimmer, you have become a fantastic skater, a fast runner, and a good hockey player who keeps improving every day.

You used to both sit at dinner making funny faces to each other. Then you would run around and play hide-and-seek and make shows and sing and dance and play with Lily, dragging her around with you. Later on, you would watch your favorite movies together, like *Shrek*, *Buzz Lightyear*, *Toy Story*, *Batman*, *Superman*, and *Spiderman*, and jump off our white leather couches and fly from the chairs to the couches and run all around the main floor in a big circle, laughing all the way.

Harrison always said, "I wish Max Librach could live beside me and our houses could be attached so I could play with him all day long."

The greatest thing that I've noticed about you and your friend Harrison is that you're both often smiling, laughing, and just all lit up together. You bring out the best in each other and enhance what is already great about each of you. And that is what friendship is all about.

Max, you found a special friend when you were just three years old, and he has changed your life. No matter what happens in life, as long as you have one really good friend, that's all you need.

I love you, Harrison. I'm so glad Max's first best friend is you.

Love, Mommy

The Magic Key: Friends are the most important gifts in your life. And a best friend is an extraspecial treasure. Also, knowing your loyalty, anyone who has you for a friend is truly blessed.

The Second Child

Different but Equally Incredible

WHEN I GOT PREGNANT with my second child, I often agonized that I could never possibly love anyone the way I loved my first. I remember saying to Cliff all the time, "How am I ever going to feel as deeply for the new baby as I do for Max?" And then Lily was born and it truly was amazing, because everything they say is true. Your heart does expand like an accordion, and the way I came to look at it is that loving Max and Lily is like loving two different genres of music. You love different things about each type of music and for different reasons, but are deeply passionate about them both. They may be different, but they are equally incredible, like two snowflakes that are each perfect in their own unique way.

We don't have as much time with a second, third, or fourth child — that's just a reality, and so as a result, we have to make that extra effort to notice them. They need it and so do you. So try to recount some of the special things and special "moments" that you shared alone with all of your children who came after the first. How were the children different? What personality traits can you tell your later children they had that were different from the first? What made them unique, not just in your eyes, but in everyone's? What did they have in common with their siblings?

Dear Lily,

You are my second child, but you are my first and only girl. Have I kept the same detailed and copious notes that I did when I only had one baby and all the time in the world? Probably not. But I experience you just as richly and as deeply as I did when I had a baby for the first time. Life is so much busier now. There's baseball and ballet, and playdates and best friends, and I feel sometimes like I'm on a treadmill and I just can't catch my breath. So we have to grab the moments when we can and really savor them. We have lots of them, and I often preface them by saying, "This is our special time together."

One day when you were two-and-a-half years old, I blew up a pink balloon that I found in one of those packages of assorted balloons. We spent about two hours just tossing that balloon back and forth to each other, and the glee and joy you experienced was a total delight to watch and enjoy. Something so simple was making you so happy. And I suspect that it wasn't only the balloon that was intoxicating you, but the total focus I had on you and that balloon for such a long time.

Being a little sister, you often had to share me with

Daily Journals — One mom had a great idea for how to write these love letters. She suggested getting two journals, one for each of her children and every night, when applicable, writing a little summary of that day's highlights and happenings. For instance, "Emily started basketball camp today" or "Sophie looked so cute in her little shin pads and her light-up running shoes that she wore to soccer." At some point later on, all these little love notes can be used to create more well-crafted love letters, but at least the memories are documented for your children's pleasure.

your big brother, so "special times" like these were a gift for you and for me. Watching you jump up in the air to catch that balloon — flicking a lock of golden hair out of your eyes, your magical tresses up in a high ponytail with wisps beside your face, framing those enormous and beautiful, luminous green eyes, your tiny little nose and perfect lips, your petite little body radiating such goodness and love — I felt my heart swell.

We tossed that balloon back and forth and it never got boring, because you were so happy, laughing and giggling and smiling that gorgeous smile of yours. That day, it was as if time stopped, and we were totally "in the moment." You gave me this chance to be present in the way we're all meant to be.

Another and probably one of our favorite special times together was every day with you at breakfast. This was often while Max slept in and we had a chance to be alone together. I love when we wake together, and we walk down the stairs and you say, "Hold my hand, Mommy" in the sweetest, most endearing way. When we get to the kitchen, I open your high chair, and these days, you're almost three, you climb into the chair all by yourself and independently do up the navy blue seat belt and then I slide in the white plastic table and make your cereal.

I also love the sameness of this activity. You have your cereal every morning, while Mommy has her whole-wheat toast and coffee, and it's a lovely little ritual that we share together.

And, of course, I love watching you have your bowl of Rice Krispies. When you are sitting in your high chair, totally absorbed in that bowl of cereal, something touches my heart. And while you're eating it, nothing else matters. You relish every single minute of it. I love that about you and I notice that how from something so simple, you are able to derive such deep satisfaction. But this is you, Lily. You are so straightforward and uncomplicated. The simple things make you happy and you enjoy them to the fullest.

One of our favorite special times together was reading a book about a mother and daughter who both wore yellow dresses. You loved that book so much that I took you to a fabric store and let you pick out this yellow cotton fabric with tiny blue flowers on it. We made mother and daughter dresses. You looked so adorable, just like the little girl in the book. I looked like a big banana in mine, but it was worth it just to make you happy, and you were so excited, you were just over the moon.

I love so many things about you, Lily, and want you to know just how unique and loved you are.

Love, Mommy

The Magic Key: Simple things often give us the chance for some of life's greatest pleasures. I love that you have given me the opportunity to know that and really get it. I love this about you. And doing something as simple as throwing a balloon up in the air or eating breakfast is magical when I do it with you.

Similar topics:

- ♥ Nursing or potty training or the pacifier the second time around.
- ♥ Older, wiser, and calmer?
- ♥ Where are the photos?
- ♥ How did you involve your older child in the experience of your new baby?

Your Masterpiece of a Love Letter

IF YOU HAD TO WRITE JUST ONE love letter right now for each child, what would you say? Write about the first time you laid eyes on your child. What do you remember about those first moments? Tell a few anecdotes that really describe what she or he means to you. Tell a story that typifies who they are, and what you love about their character and their personality. If you had to leave them with some words of motherly or fatherly wisdom, what would you say to them? And finally, tell them how much you love them and cherish them and how you will love them unconditionally forever. If you were only to write one letter per child, this is the letter to write. Make a deadline for yourself. We work best when we have a timed date whereby we have to complete the task. Write it on their birthday as a birthday letter and then save it for them. This is also an ideal letter to write to a bride on her wedding day. Moms, you can write this letter when they're little or later on, and keep it for them to present to them on or before their wedding day.

Dear Lily,

Having you in my life is like a living love letter. You are such a gift and I know that you're only on loan to me so I can take care of you and raise you and help you develop happily and healthily. Then, if you are well-adjusted and I've given you the nourishing roots you need, you will develop the wings to fly.

But I want us always to be close, and I often say to you, "I know you want to be with Mommy all the time now, but do you promise when you're older that we can still talk every day, and shop together, and go away together, and have dinners together?"

These days as I write this, you're in a Mommy phase, and when I go out lately you really cry a lot and really seem afraid. So I've been teaching you that "Mommy leaves, but Mommy always comes back." I hope you have an easy time in September when you have to separate from me for the first time. I want to help you prepare for that. I also have to prepare myself, because you're my baby and my best friend and I'm going to miss you so much when you go off to school, even if it is only five mornings a week. This summer you're going to camp, and I will be driving you there and back just like I did with Max. Mothers have asked me, "Why do you drive all the way to this camp when there's a wonderful little red bus?" But it is such special time that we can share together, and I would never give that up, because you'll remember those rides to and from camp, the sharing right after leaving camp, the picnics we'll have for lunch, and just the precious time together. I loved doing it for Max, and you used to sit in your car seat and bring your pretend knapsack along. I can't believe you're actually doing it for real now.

I love you so much that I can't think of you without my eyes welling up with tears, and yet at the same time feeling a joy and a love so deep that it taps a well I never knew existed. I remember worrying about how I was ever going to love another child, as many parents do. And it's amazing how you do. You're both so different, but I love you both equally, deeply, and passionately.

I'm going to tell you all the stories I can remember. About how happy I was that I was having a girl, about your birth, your love for the slide even more than the swing, about dolls, and books and your first best friend, and your first school and ballet and mostly about how I enjoy every minute of you.

I love that moment every day when you come down the stairs with a pretty dress and your gorgeous hairdo, and the excitement all over your face of showing everyone just how beautiful you look. And we both enjoy the moment, and it's just another delicious part of having a daughter like you. You are my dream come true and I love you with all of my heart. There's so much more to tell you. Every day with you is like opening up a jewelry box filled with beautiful, sparkling treasures, and you are the most priceless treasure of all.

Love, Mommy

The Magic Key: I know that when you read this, having the character you have, you would probably say, "And don't forget Max, Mommy. He is your other precious and priceless treasure."

Grandparents Can Do This, Too! —

The relationship between a grandparent and grandchild can be one of the most meaningful relationships in a child's life. Often, grandparents have more time to spend really listening and talking to their grandchildren. Writing love letters to your grandchildren is a wonderful idea, because it could become a great project and something your grandchild would never forget. As a journalist, I have written numerous profiles on celebrities and regular people and often the questions, "Did you have a grandparent who played a special role in your life?" or "How would you describe your grandparents or your relationship to your grandmother or grandfather?" elicit so much emotion and feeling that much of the person I am profiling is revealed in their answer about their grandparent(s). So this is a great opportunity not only for new mothers, mothers-to-be, or mothers looking back to write to their children, but for grandparents to really give a special gift of memories to them. Your perspective as a grandparent is second to none. You have wisdom, experience, and you are once removed, which gives you that big-picture perspective that parents sometimes have a harder time seeing. Your view and your observations, advice, and love are hugely valuable and would be an everlasting tribute to your love for your grandchildren.

How to Be Best Friends Forever

Advice from Mommy

ALL THE WRITING TIPS, STORIES, magic keys, and suggested topics up until now have all been geared around memories. But this is a perfect place to impart all of your wisdom, experience, life lessons, wishes, dreams, and hopes for your child. I think you could do this individually for each child, or write to them together. There is sometimes a tendency for siblings to be competitive with each other, and by encouraging them to remain close and be good friends, you are giving them a gift that they will be able to cherish forever.

What advice do you have for each of them individually? Are there any quotes or sayings that you would like to include to express your point even more? This is a letter they can really use and benefit from always, so feel free to open your heart and say everything you know that will benefit and inspire, uplift and motivate your child to be all that they can be. From the moment they were born, you had dreams for them. What are your dreams and what are your wishes? Take your magic wand and let them know.

Dear Max and Lily,
I thought it would be nice to write to both of you together. I always wanted two children for so many reasons. Naturally, I wanted to have my favourite little boy, which is you, Max, and my favourite little girl, which of course is you, Lily. But I also wanted you to always have each other. I wanted you to always have someone other than Daddy and I who would truly love you and know you and always be there for you. I want you both to promise me that you'll always be close. You'll never regret it.

Lily, please invite your brother over for dinners and look after him. Max, please protect and look after your sister always, no matter what. As Auntie Bonnie always used to say, "Zachary, if you're nice to your brother, Ely, you'll have a best friend for life; if you're not, you'll have an enemy for life." What would you choose? I know sometimes siblings can fight, but here is where I think you both come together. You both have a fabulous sense of humor and you always connect over humor and laughter. Also, you have the same history, the same relatives, and the same adoring parents.

You are each perfect in your own unique ways. But always remember to be kind to others, share what you have, help people feel good, be thoughtful, considerate, smile lots — it really does make you feel better. Always think positive and it will usually work out that way. Be cool, and don't ever give yourself away for free. Have a sense of purpose in your life, so that what you do excites and delights you. And love yourselves, so that someone really special will love you back. Laugh a lot, always have at least one best friend, and people who you care about and who care about you, and you'll always be happy.

Look after each other, help each other, be nice to each other, and love each other always. We are a family, and what I love about the four of us is that we are four pieces of a puzzle, and wherever you may be, there will always be another three. You are all my life and I love you more than you'll ever know. I hope that one day you will both have children of your own to understand the depth of feeling we have for you.

I feel sometimes like you have both given me the chance to live my life all over again, only this time I can live the fairy tale through you. If my childhood was somewhat of a flawed dress rehearsal, you are both the perfect opening night.

And remember, no matter what happens, everything always works out in the end. I love you both, with all of my heart, forever and ever. Grandma Siblin used to say to me, "My love for you knows no bounds." Because of the two of you, I finally understand what she meant.

Love, Mommy

Max's Top Ten Tips on How to Write a Love Letter to Your Children (as told to me by Max when he was six years old)

1. Write it on the computer.

2. Give some advice and make it real.

3. Use your heart in the book.

4. Try your best.

5. Try to work your hardest and then you'll get it right.

6. Ask your mom or dad for help.

7. Use real stories.

8. When you're bored or think you can't do it, just try again.

9. Always use a title, it really helps.

10. Use your periods and commas and dashes and exclamation marks and question marks.

If you do all of those things you will make a very great letter!

Acknowledgments

Have you ever heard that it takes a village to raise a child? Well, it also takes a village to help create a book. To that end, there are many people I would love to thank for helping me put this labor of love together.

The first person I have to thank is my original editor Susan Sutherland, who really helped me become a writer, and whose stringent and exacting standards were an inspiration. I also enjoyed all the meals, laughs, and great talks we shared together.

A very special thank-you to my editor and literary agent Donald Bastian for his incredible ability to make writing and editing a book an absolute joy. We laughed so much and had so much fun working together.

A special thank you to Jennifer Hale for her vision and for always "getting it" and truly caring about the concept and wanting to make it work. I also loved sharing our stories of our own children.

To Jan Christie for believing in the book and to all the friends and family who listened to the stories and supported it all these eight and a half years.

To Jill Weinstein for her friendship, laughter, support, and love in the final stages of the book when I had the daunting task of having to edit the book from 75 stories to 18. Boy, did we ever have fun!

A very special thank you to Darlene Russell, for being my teacher, coach, and friend. It is really you that I thank for helping me finally "make it happen."

To Sanja Rimarchuk, for your friendship and support.

To my family for being part of so many of the stories, to all my parents, my dad, mom, Auntie Jackie, David, Grandma Jean, and of course to my beloved late Grandma Lily Siblin. A special thanks to Evelyn and Sam, my sister Jane and brother-in-law Alen, my brothers

Eric and Steven, brothers- and sisters-in-law, Bonnie, Arthur, Mark, Heather, Rick and Carol.

A huge part of this book and of my children's lives are their beloved cousins, all of whom are part of so many of the stories. So I have to give a special hug to their loveable cousin Lewis, and to all of the Librach cousins: Zachary, Ely, Joseph, Dawn, Matthew, Adina, and Evan. And a very special thank-you to Jonah for his genuine excitement, enthusiasm, and interest in this book from the very beginning, and for that special Gameboy evening we shared at our home over the holidays. A special thank-you to all of Max and Lily's friends and all the parents of their friends, for your friendship and the joy that you bring into our lives.

There are so many people that have touched my children's lives and ours, and number one is Sa Ning, for her love, care, and total involvement in our family's happiness and well-being. You are part of our family and we thank you. Another very special thank-you goes to Olivia for her love, her humor, and even her strictness. We love and thank you, too. Thanks to both Pearls, Pearl Morgan and Pearl Harding, and a special thank you to Rina for your love, your artwork, and your lovely presence in our lives.

A special thank-you to Donna Bank and Bronwyn Shepard and everyone at the JFI for your belief in this book and all the talks, lectures, and workshops you helped to facilitate.

A special thanks to all the moms at Mumnet and to those who logged onto my Web site at www.findingyourbliss.com and to www.alovelettertomybabies.com for all of your contributions. The moms I would love to thank especially are: Deborah, Jen, Sharon, Jill, Stefanie, Samantha, Daphne, Lisa, Karen, Shelley, Alison, Laurene, Carrie, Terra, Susan, Marcy, Sari, Beverly, Celia and Maureen. Also thanks to the two dads, Cliff and Josh, for your words from the dad's point of view.

To special people along the way like Archie Schirmer for the beautiful doll for Lily, to Shri for all the karate classes, to great teachers and friends, to Espy and Sarah, and of course to Miss Nessie Grant. Thanks to Phyllis, Susan, and Rhonda for so many things.

A very special thanks to Yitz Woolf and Pushing the Envelope for the Web site design and all the support. As well, thank you to J. Michael La Fond for your photography.

A very heartfelt thank-you to my friend, the late Carol Wise, for her love, encouragement, and friendship.

A special thanks to my friends Anna K. and Antonella for Max's first haircut and for their love and friendship. Also thanks to Tula, Cherie, and Lisa.

Thanks to Wendy Peters and Karen Halpern, for making the first drop-off a success.

A very special thank-you to Lesley Sevitt, for the beautiful nursery school she had in our home, and for her love, creativity, and excellence as a pre-school educator. Also thank-you for the ballerina mirror that you and the class made for Lily.

Also thanks to Perfect Portraits, Linda Hill and Sherry Firestone for your editing and friendship. To my friends who heard the stories a million times, Marcy, Sari, and Deborah.

A special thanks to Jack David from ECW Press for believing in this book and making it possible.

And last but not least, I acknowledge my true inspiration, my two beautiful children, Max and Lily, for teaching me what love is really all about and for making my life a joy, and to my husband Cliff, for his love, support, and for everything that matters.